Hard
Is Not the
Same Thing
as Bad

Abbie Halberstadt

Illustrations by Lindsay Long

HARVEST HOUSE PUBLISHERS
EUGENE. OREGON

Interior illustrations by Lindsay Long
Cover design by Faceout Studio, Molly von Borstel
Cover photo © natrot (texture) / Shutterstock; cover illustrations by Celia Maria Baker
Interior design by Janelle Coury

For bulk, special sales, or ministry purchases, please call 1-800-547-8979.
Email: Customerservice@hhpbooks.com

Hard Is Not the Same Thing as Bad

Copyright © 2023 by Abbie Halberstadt
Published by Harvest House Publishers
Eugene, Oregon 97408
www.harvesthousepublishers.com

ISBN 978-0-7369-8675-5 (hardcover)
ISBN 978-0-7369-8676-2 (eBook)

Library of Congress Control Number: 2023931205

Printed in Colombia

23 24 25 26 27 28 29 30 31 / NI / 10 9 8 7 6 5 4 3 2

Contents

Introduction

I pressed the left side of my forehead hard against the van window, which was the only cool thing in the car. From this position, I could still watch the road and glance at the rearview mirror to see if Nola had managed to emancipate herself again from the torture device (also known as a car seat) into which I, the mother who claimed to love her and desire her best good, had so callously buckled her. Every part of my body not touching the window pulsated with heat, thanks to the sheer volume of pent-up toddler angst coupled with acute Mom Stress cohabiting an enclosed space. (I'm sharing this story with the permission of both Evy and Nola, my precious, wonderful eleven-year-old twin daughters.)

I yanked my head away from the glass as one of Nola's arms snaked free of its restraint, and she began shoving the chest clasp down toward her belly with the kind of superhuman three-year-old strength that belied her utter inability to peel the top off a yogurt cup without help. I pulled over as soon as I saw a gap in traffic, and by the time I had swan-dived over the driver's seat, impaling my own belly on the headrest (you're welcome, fellow drivers, for this brazen display of my backside), Nola had wrenched both arms free and was fumbling with the clasp at her waist.

Tears pooled in her Disney princess–sized blue eyes, adding a tragic sheen of desperation to her plight. But it was the soundtrack to all this drama—the piteous wail of betrayal emanating from her wide-open mouth—that really underscored the fact that I could do nothing to redeem myself. Nothing except free her, of course.

But that's not what I did. Instead, for the third time in fifteen minutes, I reinserted her arms into the straps, slid the buckle up to the middle of her chest, and, grimly resigned to the death of my hearing, tightened down the belt yet again.

The tenor of her wail changed as I heaved myself back into the front seat. What had been a plaintive cry became a screech of such rage that the hairs on my arms prickled with apprehension. And then the thrashing started. Soon I forgot my concern for my own eardrums and began to worry she would do herself actual harm.

Over the course of the next twenty minutes, I pulled over no fewer than four times to rebuckle her, each time pleading, praying, singing, chiding, and soothing in a vain attempt to convince my car-seat-averse daughter that staying buckled would keep her safe. By the time I parked the van in our garage and numbly slid the keys from the ignition, the conclusion to a forty-five-minute commute that should have taken twenty, Nola's shrieks had quieted slightly as her voice gave out in hoarse croaks of protest.

My chest constricted as I noticed the angry red welts on her neck from her side-to-side body slams against the straps. She was sweating and disheveled, her eyes both wild and weary. I'm sure I looked much the same. Honestly, I no longer knew what I felt. My brain had been pummeled into a bloody pulp of emotions: anger, defeat, despair, sadness for Nola, self-pity.

And dread.

Because tomorrow, I would bundle all my offspring—at the time, six kids aged nine and under—into the car, just as I usually did five days a week for our commute to the gym where I taught fitness classes. I would track down the shoes, change the diapers, fill the sippy cups, gather the snacks, and buckle all the car seats (four of them still needed help with this). And then a milder version of this tragedy would repeat itself just as it had for the last six months, except this time with more "spectators" to witness it and bear the brunt of the aural assault.

You see, I had taken only Nola in the car with me that day because the rest of the family needed a break from at least one source of toddler histrionics. The plan had worked beautifully for everyone who stayed home with my husband, Shaun, but backfired in a big way for me and Nola, since none of her brothers or sisters were present to distract her from her loathing for her car seat.

We were all well versed in misdirection after half a year of doing our best to keep the twinsies from shooting off like emotional rockets each time we all piled in the car to go to the gym or the grocery store or to church. Believe me: There were times I genuinely considered never leaving the house again. Nola's identical twin sister, Evy, was usually right beside her, egged on by her twin's rallying cries of dissent, matching her scream for scream. If Nola was the ringleader of this circus, Evy was her star performer.

As I walked inside, cradling Nola's now limp, quiet form, one stark chorus beat a tattoo against my battered brain: "I hate this. This is hard. I hate this. This is so, so hard."

It was not my finest mothering moment. But it was honest.

In that exact moment, I could see no point to this daily liturgy of meltdowns in the car. The girls were in a hard stage, and tantrums happened at home as well, but there was something especially crazy-making about the inability to face my girls, to hold their cheeks in my hands and breathe with them, to escape from the sheer incessancy of their shrieks for even a moment.

"Why, Lord," I prayed, "would You put me through this kind of nonsense when it diminishes my capacity to mother my other kids well and takes so much mental energy to face each day?"

I had been repeating some version of this prayer for months—had prayed it in the past during other trying seasons—and the Lord had always been gracious to answer me eventually. But this time, I barely made it through the mudroom door before I had my answer (not in an audible voice but just about): "What part of my death on the cross for your sins was easy? And yet, behold, what good has come of it."

I froze, and Nola raised her head to gaze at me in concern as I stood, tears in my eyes now, contemplating this perspective that felt like both an old friend (because this was not my first rodeo with toddler tantrums) and a startling revelation.

What if my twin girls' seemingly meaningless melodramas were not a punishment but rather a mercy from the Lord? A daily opportunity to die to myself? To root out impatience and self-indulgence. To grow my capacity for both empathy and tenacity. To make me a more creative mama. And ultimately, to drive me to my knees at the foot of the hard, painful, bloody cross my Savior endured, not randomly or without purpose but for my ultimate benefit.

What if good could come from being dragged through the emotional wringer on the daily? What if, instead of despising the hard and kicking at it in contempt and disgust, I embraced it with open, if faltering, arms and leaned into its potential to transform my view of God and of His goodness in allowing me to walk a difficult path? What if I truly let myself believe that hard is not the same thing as bad?

 What if I truly let myself believe that hard is not the same thing as bad?

1

A Tiny Perspective Shift

REAPING THE BENEFITS OF LOOKING AT HARD A WHOLE NEW WAY

I would love to tell you that my mudroom epiphany cured me of all impatience, selfishness, and desire for control. That it transformed me from a woman who cringed at the prospect of being trapped in the van for an hour with the twins' hysterics to one who drowned them out by joyfully belting out, "Shout to the Lord."

But I think we both know I'd be lying (although, truthfully, the older kids and I did quite a bit of boisterous hymn singing to distract the twins from their woes).

A Life Preserver of Truth

What that moment in the mudroom did accomplish, however, was to furnish me with a life preserver, a simple truth to buoy me when I found myself slipping beneath the choppy waters of another deafening car ride, followed by a forty-minute episode of two little girls acting as if eating my *delicious* (just ask their siblings) homemade spaghetti sauce was akin to my smashing their cute little toes one at a time with a hammer, followed by a fight to the death over pajamas—all while Shaun was gone on a work trip.

"Just because this is hard," I reminded myself, "does not mean it's bad. The Lord is doing a good work in me, and He's going to complete it…eventually (Philippians 1:6). He's upholding me with His righteous right hand (Isaiah 41:10). I will reap a good harvest if I do not give up (Galatians 6:9)."

I'm not a mantra girl. More like a Scripture girl (see above). But sometimes just muttering, "Hard is not the same thing as bad," under my breath was the tiny perspective shift that allowed me to view my girls' synchronized fits not as a personal attack on my sanity but as a chance for professional motherhood development. I reminded myself that only the most elite athletes win the gold, and only the most dedicated soldiers earn the prestigious Medal of Honor.

Victors, Not Victims

What both have in common is an intimate knowledge of the kind of hard that eats just about every other version of the concept for breakfast. It's no accident that the Bible compares the whole of Christian life to both a race and a battle. Second Timothy 4:7 says, "I have fought the good fight, I have finished the race, I have kept the faith." If that's not "hard is not the same thing as bad" summed up in a single verse, I don't know what is. Above all, this little phrase (and all the biblical truth that undergirds it) upended the narrative that I was a victim of my twins' mood swings and car seat catastrophes.

A friend (we'll call her Kim) once described her shock when her third child bucked everything she thought she knew about parenting. Her first two were compliant and sweet-natured. She was convinced she had aced her motherhood exam. However, her third, a daughter, ripped my friend's Super Mom cape right off her shoulders, stomped on it, and then hacked it up with her mom's best scissors just for good measure. Kim had assumed no child would do the things

I have fought the good fight, I have finished the race, I have kept the faith.

2 TIMOTHY 4:7

her third born did—kicking, screaming, biting, throwing herself on the ground, intentionally hurting her siblings—unless she was taught to.

Not so.

"I learned so much about human depravity (that I hadn't wanted to acknowledge) from both my daughter's feral actions and my own angry reactions," she said. Counselors told her to put her little girl on strong medication to sedate her wild behavior, and my friend begged her husband to let her put her daughter under the care of a professional who might be more successful in taming her ways.

He said no.

"I told him she was ruining the peace of my home, but God made it evident to me, over time, that it was not my out-of-control daughter who was wrecking our home's peace. She was just being a sinful child. It was my rage-filled reactions, as the adult in the scenario, that were the main peace stealers. God was so gracious to teach me, through each battle royale with my girl, how desperately I needed Him and how much the victory belonged to Him, not me."

Only when Kim acknowledged that she was not the victim of a four-year-old—not because of her exceptional parenting skills but because God was using her parenting weaknesses to teach her about *His* sufficiency—did she begin to see breakthroughs in her connection with her daughter. Eventually, she found herself thanking her Creator for blessing her with such a wild child to give her a fresher, humbler perspective on motherhood and the ways the hard things in it grow us and shape us in Christ's image.

The best part? That little girl is now twenty years old, and she is one of the most delightful, tenderhearted, hardworking young women I have ever had the pleasure to meet. Her countenance is beautiful and serene, and her parents credit her with spiritual insight beyond her years. Kim actually told me, "I want to be like her when I grow up." This sweet mama is so grateful the Lord kept her from buckling beneath the weight of those initial hard years and from listening to either the "professional" advice or her own desire for a calm, frictionless household.

Only Jesus Is Enough

So much of my friend's story resonated with me, with a few tweaks. If you've read my book *M Is for Mama*, then you know that Ezra, our firstborn, took me on a yearlong not-so-merry chase through the wilds of potty training that disabused me of any notion of superior parenting or perfect methods. So by the time Evy and Nola (who had been easy, cherubic babies) began their descent into the Tyranny of Toddlerhood, I doubted I was still harboring any delusions of mothering grandeur. I thought I could handle hard with the best of them, not because I was so great but because I had learned to be tough in Christ's strength. All you had to do was grit your teeth, hang on for the ride, and pray your way to the end of it.

What I hadn't accounted for was just how much more nerve-grating the results of an emotional breakdown were when you doubled the recipe. One headstrong child depletes you. Two suck you bone dry. Or so I told myself in the early stages of the girls' passionate struggles with, well, most things. There were times I was convinced their behavior would hollow me out, leaving behind a mere husk of my formerly resilient self.

Did you catch the last bit? *My* resilient self.

Clearly, I still had not mastered the art of leaning heavily on the staff of Christ's enoughness in times of stress. It was truly the Lord's reminding me of Jesus's response to hard—"Who for the joy that was set before him endured the cross, despising the shame, and is seated at the right hand of the throne of God" (Hebrews 12:2)—that shifted my eyes from all the teeth gritting, bootstrapping, and bullet praying to a higher goal.

Could I somehow fix my eyes on a future joy and endure my own small cross with anything like the equanimity of my Savior? Was something more than survival possible in this scenario?

In my own strength? No.

But as God began, day by day, to nudge my perspective further away from "making it" and nearer to a picture only He could provide of what my sweet, strong-willed twinsies (and I) could one day become, I felt the muscles of my back begin to uncoil for the first time in months.

If you're hoping for a Cinderella story of transformation at this point, I'm going to disappoint you. No amount of bibbidi-bobbidi-boo would have had any material effect on Evy and Nola's theatrical tendencies. In fact, so much of the time, their poofy Cinderella dresses were a significant contributor to the problem, since nothing tipped them over the edge more quickly than having their beloved tulle skirts smooshed down by car seat buckles (nothing except being told to change out of said princess dresses in the first place, that is).

The Slow Road to Sanity

But I had been injected with a fresh vision for our future, and I trusted from experience that the Lord would be faithful to fill in the inevitable gaps in my resolve and application. Over the next year (yep, you read that right), we worked with the twinsies daily to teach them how to manage their emotions (lots of redirection, rephrasing, disciplining, breathing, praying, and repetition), took practical steps to avoid certain triggers (you better believe I donated a fluffy skirt or four), and became even more creative with our misdirection techniques. We even created a mythical creature called a "pink and purple polka-dotted fuzzy-wiggle." The older kids became professionals at "sighting" the elusive beasts at the most crucial moments of distraction from near meltdowns, and even though the twins quickly caught on to the joke, they still loved to crane their necks for a glimpse as part of the silly fun.

 *I had been injected with a fresh vision for our future, and I trusted from experience that the Lord would be faithful to fill in the inevitable gaps in my resolve and application.*

Gradually, we saw improvement in the quality of our daily commute, but it wasn't until we were a few months away from their fourth birthday that I had the sudden blessed realization, driving in the car with all six kids on board, that no one was screaming. Praises be! For the first time in more days than I could begin to count, we had peacefully loaded the car, trekked down the driveway (the point when the first sputters of protest usually started), and driven to the gym.

Turning four was a tipping point toward maturity for the girls, and it was a good thing too, since I was six months pregnant with our seventh baby, Honor, and we were chin deep in the process of building our second DIY house from scratch. Twin toddler angst is stressful. Twin toddler angst plus pregnancy plus housebuilding is like saying "Here, hold my anvil" to a drowning woman.

Not only that, but we'd just begun a journey through the most traumatic friendship breakup we've ever experienced (more on that later).

Refining and Restoring

Turns out asking the Lord to grow your capacity for hard is a bit like praying for patience: You might not like what He "puts you through" in answer to your prayer. Still, He was so gracious to bring us out of that season of intense highs and lows with the twinsies just as we entered a new season of challenges and heartbreaks. We see this principle of refining, then restoring (then refining again) in 1 Peter 5:10: "And after you have suffered a little while, the God of all grace, who has called you to his eternal glory in Christ, will himself restore, confirm, strengthen, and establish you." I can look back now and see His impeccable timing in allowing what He did when He did, even if I couldn't fathom the reasons in the midst of deeply painful moments of experiencing rejection in friendship.

Turns out asking the Lord to grow your capacity for hard is a bit like praying for patience: You might not like what He "puts you through" in answer to your prayer.

Neither could I have grasped just how far from those days of tantrums and tears the Lord would carry my twin girls. Since they are still just eleven, I have only been privileged to peek at the heights of greatness to which God will take them, but if their personalities at the moment are any indication, it's going to be Mount Everest–level epic.

A Glimmer of Hope

Evy and Nola are the glimmer of hope I love to offer all young mamas because their cheerfulness, sensitivity, gentleness with children, generosity, and adventurous palates *now* would have you imagining them as the kinds of toddlers who shared their toys with all and docilely ate whatever you put on their plates. (The truth is, for a while there, we chanted and cheered ourselves hoarse on a nightly basis to coax either girl into eating even a bite of dinner.)

I've had some compliant small children too, and, while the twinsies were no such specimens, I can see now how their finely (over)tuned emotional natures poised them to be the most empathetic of souls (once said natures had marinated in a God-given concoction of time and prayer and training, of course). I know this is what you're supposed to say, but I would truly change nothing about their hard toddler years, not only because they make me appreciate their fun, snuggly, sparkly personalities all the more now but also because their toddlerhood prepared me to be relatively unfazed by the more difficult stages of the siblings who followed them.

One of their younger brothers struggled with "rage monster" issues for almost two years. (I'll share some of how we helped him through that later.) Another regressed on potty training for months. Yet another alternated between losing his mind over every single step of bedtime or lunchtime or naptime or insert-any-word-you'd-like-time and displaying the kind of cheerful (and not-so-cheerful) obstinacy that looks you square in the face as you give him instructions and then does the complete opposite.

Did I love any of these phases? Did I do "spirit sprinkles" and shout, "Huzzah, he's disobeying again"?

Of course not.

I'm a mother, not a character in an *SNL* skit.

Did I sometimes text my husband while he was traveling for work and wearily admit that I'd just said out loud to myself while doing laundry, "I don't like _____ very much right now"?

Yep. I'm only human.

But I'll tell you this: None of these phases tied me up in knots the same way Evy and Nola's double struggles did—for one very simple reason. When you've dealt with daily eruptions of Mount Twindom, getting blasted by only one little volcano feels a bit (if only a little bit) ho-hum. (This is not a knock on singleton mamas. I am one, and I will never deny that one strong-willed child is *hard*. But having twins tweaked the way I view my hard, and perspective shifts are kind of the point I'm making, after all.)

Even more, because of the protracted nature of the twins' high-strung phase, I'd had hundreds of back-to-back days to practice the art of allowing the Holy Spirit to grow me in the fruit of the Spirit. I had *so* far to go (still do), but praise God, He never leaves us exactly where He finds us!

A Different Kind of "Gains"

As I navigated each new kind of "kid hard" the Lord placed in my path, I became aware I was flexing different, stronger, and more Christ-reliant spiritual muscles than I'd been using with the twinsies. On top of that, I genuinely wasn't as bothered by the hard. Sometimes I was even able to thank God for it in the moments it was happening! It was a real-life fleshing out of Colossians 2:6-7 (NASB): "Therefore, as you have received Christ Jesus the Lord, so walk in Him, having been firmly rooted and now being built up in Him and established in your faith, just as you were instructed, and overflowing with gratitude."

Even now, as I'm parenting another set of twin three-year-olds, the challenges, while present, don't produce the same anxiety as they did before.

That tiny perspective shift I mentioned at the beginning of this chapter has borne so much fruit in my life, my husband's life, and our family's life by extension. And it has been all the sweeter knowing it was Christ's work in me, not my own "toughness," that made the change.

DAD THOUGHT

Hi, Shaun here. When Abbie asked me if I would contribute to this book, I wasn't sure what I could tell a bunch of mamas about motherhood that wouldn't come across like a dog telling a cat how to purr. So I'm not going to do that. I'll leave the *purr*fect (sorry, this is a dad thought—I had to) mamahood encouragement to Abbie and will instead provide a father's insight on "hard is not the same thing as bad" in hopes of adding another layer of perspective that will help both mothers and fathers encourage each other to lean into the Lord when the going gets tough.

Meow on to my thoughts on that tiny perspective shift Abbie was talking about.

At first glance, it might not seem like dads would need as much encouragement to dig deep into the hard parts of parenting. After all, in a traditional breadwinner/homemaker breakdown, we're not usually the ones putting in as many hours with the kids as our wives. On top of that, in other areas we're supposed to be the stoic ones—the ones who take pride in conquering the highest peaks, surviving the harshest conditions, and subduing our greatest fears. "Hard"—at least in terms of feats—is practically what we crave and certainly what we measure each other against. How else could so many competitive survival shows succeed on cable television?

Yet when you switch from those individualistic "man versus cruel world" endeavors to the realm of daily consistency, relationship building, and service in marriage and fatherhood—well, let's just say *that* version of hard doesn't look nearly as appealing or rewarding.

After all, what man would ever want to watch husbands compete over diaper changing, bedtime stories, midnight feedings, and devotions with their kids?

Here, in the daily struggle, is where fathers most need the perspective shift, so they can see those often unheralded (yet invaluable) rewards that God has in store for those who honor Him in their family life. The good news? Dads are likely already predisposed to pursue physically hard things. We just need encouragement to channel that energy into the "small" tasks of parenthood where we can discover a hard that is truly worthy of pursuit.

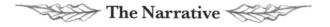 **The Narrative**

THE WORLD'S RESPONSE TO HARD	A CHRISTIAN RESPONSE TO HARD
Believes we are victims of the ways our kids "treat" us	Believes that through Christ, we always have the choice to overcome
Says that someone more patient would do this better	Is confident that God equips us with what we need when we need it
Is convinced that the longer the hard phase is, the worse it is	Knows that quick fixes rarely produce good character

 **Action Steps**

- Memorize and meditate on 2 Timothy 4:7: "I have fought the good fight, I have finished the race, I have kept the faith."
- Write five sticky notes with "hard ≠ bad" on them and post them in high-traffic areas of your home as reminders of this tiny perspective shift.
- Pray about one friend who could help hold you accountable in changing the way you view the hard things in motherhood. Reach out when the Lord brings someone to mind.

Questions

Do I view hard primarily as bad?

If so, am I getting this view from worldly culture or the Bible?

What is something hard in motherhood right now that the Lord is also using for good? And how?

Prayer

Lord, thank You that Jesus "for the joy that was set before him endured the cross, despising the shame" (Hebrews 12:2), and, in the process, set the ultimate example of hard not being the same thing as bad. Help us to shift our mindsets from negativity to joy in You by Your strength.

2

Hard Things
Are Not Always
Suffering

KEEPING PERSPECTIVE IN THE
MIDST OF THE STRUGGLE

I can just hear some of you who resonated with the beginning of this book: "Man, it's like she's speaking straight to me. The crazy has been strong with my toddler lately. I feel so seen!"

But I also imagine there are more than a few of you thinking, "It's been a while since I've been in the toddler stage. I mean, I remember the struggle, but surely this isn't the hardest thing this lady's been through."

Or maybe even: "What about true suffering? Cancer? Betrayal? Chronically ill kids? When is she going to get to the deep stuff?"

Not Everyone Struggles the Same Way

All of these perfectly legitimate responses illustrate a universal tendency—the oh-so-human desire to see our own circumstances reflected back to us in the lived experience of those from whom we seek comfort and advice.

I lost count long ago of the number of messages I've received through social media that say things like "What do you do when your special-needs child takes up so much more time than your other kids?" even though I do not have a special-needs child. Or "When your husband treats you in such and such a way, how do you respond?" when I have not experienced the particular kind of behavior they describe.

I'll be honest: These kinds of messages used to flummox me, not because I didn't believe there were helpful principles (or sympathy) I could offer but because they come from the erroneous assumption that everyone has booked a ticket on the exact same struggle bus. I have had to learn and remind myself often that, for many of us, when we're hurting, our suffering is too all-encompassing to fathom anyone else's reality without it.

So if you're here looking for a mirror of your tragic life circumstances, you may find it in some chapters but not in others. If you're searching for a step-by-step for how to cope with the pain of an adult child gone astray, you may find hope in Christ but not the unique-to-your-exact-scenario salve you crave (because I do not yet have adult children). If you're wondering how to survive the death of a beloved family member, you may glean biblical wisdom but still feel the sting of loss.

Suffering Versus Challenge

I've *absolutely* wrestled with much more challenging trials than twin toddler meltdowns, and I'll share more about those hard scenarios throughout this book. But I feel compelled to say something up front: This is not primarily a book about suffering but about the common knee-jerk tendency to slap a negative label on any form of adversity right before we sprint away from it as if a grizzly bear is hot on our tail. (Or, if that's too much effort, we numb ourselves to it with wine and reality TV.)

All suffering is hard. But not all hard things are suffering.

The *Oxford English Dictionary* says that to suffer is to "experience or be subjected to (something bad or unpleasant)."

Conversely, a challenge is a "task or situation that tests someone's abilities."

That's a crucial distinction to make, *especially* when I'm seeking, first and foremost, to tackle the question of how to find the good in those testing circumstances rather than to solve the conundrum of why some of us suffer more than others.

A Biblical Response to Hard

Thankfully, the Bible has much to say about what our response to difficulty should be. Take, for instance, how the Lord tells Joshua to "be strong and courageous" no fewer than three times in as many verses (Joshua 1:6, 7, 9) as He gives ol' Josh the daunting task of driving the pagan peoples from the Promised Land. God requires similarly valiant and trusting responses from Noah, Esther, David, Ruth, Abraham, Isaiah, Hosea, and so many more. You could even say that booting His children right out of their comfort zones is a bit of a biblical theme.

My goal is always to return to the truth of Scripture, no matter how far into the weeds of worldly culture we have strayed. So if you opened this book hoping for encouragement that even though motherhood is hard, we can do hard things in Christ's strength (just like the ordinary people I've mentioned above!), with His Word as our guide, then you are in the right place.

One of the reasons I feel compelled to lay out so clearly the differences between hard things and suffering is that popular motherhood messaging hammers us with the assurance that much of what we encounter from our children on a daily basis is not merely a challenge but instead true affliction.

I get it! I coined the term "emotional terrorist" in our home for those moments when the three-year-old is leveraging every bit of his lung capacity, his mess-making prowess, and his iron will to intentionally torpedo my day.

Or at least that's what it can seem like he's doing when my focus rests solely on the disruption to *my* peace, the injury to *my* feelings, and the upending of *my* neat little plan for the day. But regardless of how hard my emotions work to convince me I'm justified in my disdain for this pint-sized impediment to either my productivity or my relaxation, Scripture tells a different story.

A Manifesto on Contentment

In one of the most quoted yet least understood verses in the Bible, Paul says, "I can do all things through Christ who strengthens me" (Philippians 4:13 NKJV). Athletes tattoo it on their bodies. College students scribble it at the top of their final exam papers. But this is not a verse about impressive feats of brains or brawn. It is, instead, a manifesto on contentment. Sure, Paul can do "all things" through Christ. But what "things" exactly? Well, having money. Or not having money. Eating well. Or going without. Lacking nothing. Or lacking everything. I'm paraphrasing, of course, but this is the exact quote that sums it all up: "I have learned the secret of being content in any and every situation" (Philippians 4:12 NIV). So that means when the baby sleeps, or when he wakes up seven times. When the teenager participates with a helpful attitude, or when he drags his feet and mutters under his breath. When the nine-year-old cleans up after her muffin baking, or when she drops a flour grenade on the kitchen floor and walks away.

Well, shoot.

You mean, we're not victims of our children's tendency to upchuck an entire lunch of undigested chicken quesadillas an hour into a road trip? Of their propensity to embarrass us in public with the way they parrot our impatient tones? Of their fondness for smashing that one heirloom dish we asked them never to touch?

Short answer? No, we're not.

A Motherhood of Martyrdom

Our children are not "something bad or unpleasant we are being subjected to," to borrow from the above definition of suffering. And yet when we view dealing with their more challenging traits as suffering rather than as a hard-but-good opportunity to grow in Christlikeness, we gravitate toward a Motherhood of Martyrdom—an attitude sure to bleed into the way we treat our families.

As one reader so poignantly put it, "My mother made sure to let us know we were a martyrdom she barely survived. It has been really depressing for us children."

I don't doubt it. Few things crush my spirit *as an adult* more than being made to feel like a burden, and I'm so glad my own mother understood the importance of regularly speaking to my brother and me with the kind of language that let us know just how wanted and loved and *unburdensome* we were.

Maybe you're thinking, "But, Abbie. I *don't* think of myself as a martyr. I know that children are a blessing. I rarely watch TV, much less the trashy kind. And I don't need alcohol to make it through the day. Is this really something I need to hear?"

Perhaps not. But I do have a couple of questions for you: Do you respond to your children's constant use of the four-letter word "Mama" with a huff sometimes? Do you feel offended when you walk into the laundry room to discover the chaotic evidence of little hands rifling through clean clothes in search of that favorite threadbare T-shirt? Do you "mention" the overflowing trash bin to your fourteen-year-old in a less-than-patient tone?

Confession: I chose these examples because they are all things I have done *in the last week*. And this despite the fact that I don't watch junk TV, don't drink, and do believe children are a blessing. (Sidenote: Though a teetotaler myself, I have no problem with alcohol consumption in moderation, but I have concerns when I see it touted far too often as the means by which we "cope with life.") So far, so good, I suppose. Problem is, it doesn't really matter how many doing-it-right boxes we tick if our heart attitudes are still ones of resentment or impatience. To paraphrase a line from *M Is for Mama*, the ultimate issue with our mothering struggles is not our bad days or our hormones but instead our inability to be anything other than mediocre without Christ.

We Do Not Lose Heart

Without a biblical perspective on hard things, we will default to a cheap contentment that only sighs with relief when our circumstances match our desires (which, let's be honest, is no contentment at all). Or we will chafe at even the

So we do not lose heart.
Though our outer self is
wasting away, our inner
self is being renewed
day by day.
2 CORINTHIANS 4:16

barest suggestion that we do not *deserve* to begrudge the really gnarly parts of motherhood. You know, the stuff we simply don't enjoy one single bit.

Not only that, but the more we muddle true suffering with hard mothering days, the less likely we are to find comfort in verses like 2 Corinthians 4:16-18, which says, "So we do not lose heart. Though our outer self is wasting away, our inner self is being renewed day by day. For this light momentary affliction is preparing for us an eternal weight of glory beyond all comparison, as we look not to the things that are seen but to the things that are unseen. For the things that are seen are transient, but the things that are unseen are eternal."

As a breastfeeding mama, I couldn't help but giggle at that "outer self wasting away" part. Anybody else ever weaned a baby, only to look down at your sad, deflated chest and think, "RIP, perky boobs—it was fun while it lasted"? Motherhood has very real, very obvious "wasting" effects on our bodies. And yet when our attitude is one of joyfully looking for the good, not one stretch mark or varicose vein (of which I have plenty) is, well, wasted.

Choosing to Speak Life

On social media, I regularly address the topic of speaking words of life over our children, regardless of how hard a day we've had, and I am typically met with one of two responses: (1) hearty agreement or (2) outrage at the perceived marginalization of the hard things in motherhood.

One woman who stumbled upon a post of mine on just this subject made the statement that choosing to actively limit words of complaining or snark was the "reason why mothers commit suicide." Motherhood is hard, she said. To that I say, *Amen!* But I cannot agree that encouraging ourselves and others to see and speak the good is false and damaging (I'll talk more about why soon).

I did not glean enough information about this woman to know whether she is a Christian, but I got the strong impression she would not label herself as such. So it comes as no surprise that she did not resonate with my description of her overwhelm as a "light and momentary affliction" that could help prepare her for an eternity of joy. It was, in fact, *offensive* to her. (After all, 1 Peter 2:7-8 describes Jesus as a "rock of offense" over which unbelievers stumble.) When we are deep in the trenches of motherhood, little feels more insulting than the implication that choosing joy in Christ is the ladder that will lead to our freedom. The freedom part sounds nice, but it couldn't possibly be that simple (I said nothing about easy).

Oh, but it could. And it is. One of the most miraculous things that walking with Christ does for every believing mama who will receive its gift is to grant us not only a right view of hardship but also the strength to choose that perspective day after day instead of defaulting to victim status.

 One of the most miraculous things that walking with Christ does for every believing mama who will receive its gift is to grant us not only a right view of hardship but also the strength to choose that perspective day after day instead of defaulting to victim status.

Suffering is real. Hard things are inevitable. But conflating the two within the context of motherhood is a surefire way to "lose heart" and lose sight of the unique opportunity every hard day gives us to throw ourselves onto the safety net of Jesus's new morning mercies, firm in the knowledge that it will never break.

When I mentioned in the last chapter that we dads have a drive to endure and conquer hard things, I'm guessing some of you mamas thought of the last time a Man Cold laid your husband out on the couch, leaving him too incapacitated to change diapers or help put kids to bed.

Of course, the irony is that the very same "debilitating" sickness would never keep him from a camping trip if he really wanted to go. He would, in fact, consider himself even manlier for enduring it.

So why the inconsistency?

Because we men can't let a good Man Cold go to waste! We possess a seemingly paradoxical tendency to take pride in or employ our hardship and suffering for our own gain. After all, the sicker I was while I climbed the mountain, the more impressive the achievement. And the sicker I am at home, the more likely it is my wife will make those comfort foods I love so much *while* I avoid dealing with the bedtime battle.

The thing is, this tendency certainly isn't unique to fathers. Remember when your toddler scratched his finger, and it was going to fall right off unless he got a hug, a kiss, four Spider-Man Band-Aids, some ice cream, and...(your toddler will certainly have a suggestion or three to complete the thought).

We humans learn young and require zero instruction on the art of exaggerating our suffering to maximize attention, comfort, and treats. I'm guessing you can think of instances, in the hardest seasons of mothering, in which this holds true for you too. The problem is, in the same way "number two" face is only endearing on a baby, playing up the hard doesn't look nearly as cute on a grown-up who should know better.

Adults are *supposed* to have learned selflessness. It benefits no one but ourselves to exaggerate our suffering. In fact, it adds to our spouses' load. To sum it up for the dads, Man Colds beget Mama Overwork.

Not that we refuse to acknowledge suffering. It's only natural to desire help, comfort, and attention when we're struggling. And it is good and right to offer solace to those in need. However, we must be honest about the severity of our plight, not making it out to be worse or better than it is, lest we allow our self-centeredness to burden the ones we love or rob them of an opportunity to show their love for us.

 **The Narrative**

THE WORLD'S RESPONSE TO HARD	A CHRISTIAN RESPONSE TO HARD
Views all hardship as suffering	Knows that some hard things are simply challenges, which can produce great benefits in our lives
Believes that motherhood often equals martyrdom	Believes motherhood is a (hard, but good) gift
Makes the goal to "get through" the hard things as quickly as possible	Understands that hardship in this life is brief and fleeting compared to the weight of eternal glory we have in store for us

 **Action Steps**

- Memorize and meditate on 2 Corinthians 4:16: "So we do not lose heart. Though our outer self is wasting away, our inner self is being renewed day by day."

- Write down two things you have viewed as suffering that are actually just God-given challenges.

- Ask your accountability partner from the last chapter to pray for you to view these two struggles rightly as you mother this week.

Questions

Why (biblically) does God allow us to experience hard things?

How does viewing hard things as the challenges they are (instead of viewing them as suffering) materially affect the way I treat my children?

What are two specific ways I can grow in Christlikeness through the challenges I'm experiencing?

Prayer

Lord, thank You that we really can do "all things through Christ who strengthens [us]" (Philippians 4:13 NKJV)—including finding contentment in hard circumstances. Grant us eyes to see the opportunities for sanctification and growth tucked inside each new mothering challenge we encounter.

3

The Problem with Easy

GROWTH REQUIRES STRUGGLE

I rarely use social media for personal purposes anymore. I share family pictures on my blog channels, but I cannot seem to find the time to curate an entirely different set of memories and experiences for a personal account.

Before I started blogging, though, I posted snippets of our daily life with one, then two, then three small children to Facebook. So now, when I log in to check on my blog page, my personal account regularly reminds me of posts I wrote over a decade ago. Usually, I love seeing the throwback pictures and reminiscing about the adorable turns of phrase my oldest son used or the way my daughter's chestnut curls swirled around her shoulders on her *first birthday* (girlfriend basically had Pantene model status from birth).

Not a "Natural Mother"

One day, though, I stopped short as I read my one-line update. It said, "I get inordinately frustrated by how long it takes small children to do anything."

There was no explanation, no context, no accompanying photo of a cute, turtle-paced five-year-old fumbling with his shoelaces. Just a stark confession of my impatience in fourteen black words on a white screen. I don't remember writing those exact words, but I distinctly remember experiencing that annoyance. I have one older brother, so I didn't grow up around young children, and I am not a "naturally patient person" (despite the regular assumption to the contrary when people find out how many kids I have).

In fact, my predisposition toward toddler intolerance can be illustrated with a quick anecdote. One summer, when I was twelve, I visited a family with seven kids, and one day, after a game of water hose tag on the trampoline, we all sat down in a circle to play Duck, Duck, Goose. I watched in concern as the two-year-old backed his dripping, grass-covered caboose toward me. Before I could scramble away, he plopped right down on my lap.

And I recoiled in disgust.

Now, to be fair, I don't know too many people who love being sat on by a sopping wet toddler. But I also know that my lack of experience plus natural personality bent set me up for an inevitable response of "Ew, get off." (I didn't say it out loud, but it was written plainly in my grimace and stiff posture.)

So how in the world did this small-child-averse preteen end up with so many kids? Hang on. I'm getting there.

A Changed Heart

You might be surprised to hear that when people ask which number (as in, amount) of children has been the hardest for me and my husband, Shaun, we both immediately say, "Two!"

Not five. Not eight. Not even ten.

But two.

Why? Because when we "only" had two small children, neither of us had yet learned many of the valuable lessons and skills we now have in our parenting toolbox, and both of our sons' hard phases seemed endless. We wondered if they would ever potty train, talk, learn to buckle their own car seats, regulate *any* of their own emotions, wipe their own bums, or (when they did finally learn to wipe them) refrain from using an entire roll of toilet paper per bathroom session.

That uncertainty about whether anything we were doing would ever be effective made us antsy. We were ready to start seeing results! C'mon, fellas. Let's get to the self-sufficient stage already, shall we?

Fast-forward to now, when my children have vomited, peed, pooped, bled, and snotted on me too many times to number. The mundane antics of small children, however gross, barely register much of the time. And my children's developmental phases usually don't, ahem, faze me. (And I type this sentence *with* one of my twin toddlers slapping my chest and happily screeching at me while sitting on my lap.)

So what changed?

I did, by the grace of God.

Romans 12:1-2 says, "I appeal to you therefore, brothers, by the mercies of God, to present your bodies as a living sacrifice, holy and acceptable to God, which is your spiritual worship. Do not be conformed to this world, but be transformed by the renewal of your mind, that by testing you may discern what is the will of God, what is good and acceptable and perfect."

Spoiler alert: God's good, acceptable, and perfect will for every Christian is to be "transformed into his image with ever-increasing glory, which comes from the Lord, who is the Spirit" (2 Corinthians 3:18 NIV). The unique methods He uses to effect this transformation will vary, but I'd wager that, just like we talked about in the last chapter, every Jesus-loving mama, regardless of how she has received her children (biologically or through adoption), would agree that motherhood is a profession rife with opportunities to offer our bodies as "living sacrifices."

Transformation Requires Struggle

I was already a believer before I became a mother. I had encountered physical pain and struggles. But they were nothing compared to the exquisite agony of the "ring of fire" during an unmedicated vaginal home birth. They were child's play compared to the time an ob-gyn disappeared up to her *elbows* inside my womb in her efforts to turn and deliver a transverse twin—and this *after* the one and only epidural I have ever gotten wore off my nether regions. They were negligible compared with the pain of cracked, bleeding nipples and afterbirth cramps that rivaled transition contractions. They were laughable when pitted against the sleep deprivation of twins who woke up five times a night each on opposite schedules.

On top of that, the "simple" process of rolling from one side to the other while forty-two weeks pregnant can be quite the act of "spiritual worship" when we look at it through the Romans 12 lens of being willing to forgo our own comfort for the sake of obedience to God's will. (And I've gone to forty-two-plus weeks five times!)

So why, when Scripture so clearly teaches that transformation requires struggle, are we quick to bypass the hard if an easier way exists? We opt for the epidural (remember, I had one of those with my second set of twins—no judgment here). We pop pain pills at the slightest twinge. We switch to a bottle in the midst of the nipples-that-resemble-ground-hamburger episodes (not hating on bottles—I'm just making a point).

Easier Feels Better (Even When It's Not)

The most obvious answer is that easier feels better. It also requires less effort. And time. And sacrifice.

Come to think of it, easy is sounding pretty good, right? It sure is! And let me tell you: Easy can be better than good. Easy, happy babies are wonderful breaks from fussy, colicky ones. Easy, personable teenagers are a welcome relief from sullen preteens. Easy, uncomplicated pregnancies can redeem the miserable ones. Seasons of ease are not wrong or bad any more than hard ones are. They are good gifts from God.

But when easy becomes our default or our expectation in most, if not all, scenarios, we have a problem.

COUNT IT ALL JOY... WHEN YOU MEET TRIALS OF VARIOUS KINDS.

JAMES 1:2

When easy becomes our default or our expectation in most, if not all, scenarios, we have a problem.

And it's a problem so pervasive in our society that the mere suggestion of mothering "the hard way," however that looks for each of us—or even having children at all—is met with contempt and even aggression, despite the fact that God calls us to embrace the struggle (James 1:2-3) and allow the difficulty to produce fruit both in us and in the children He gives us.

We Get to Set the Tone

I've received dozens of messages over the years asking some version of the following: "How do you announce a pregnancy when your family members (or friends or co-workers or neighbors) don't understand why you would choose to be pregnant at all? They don't get why you would 'do this to yourself,' and so they respond with unkindness. What do you say?"

In fact, I answered the question so many times that, after we had our eighth baby, I wrote a blog entry about it so I could simply direct new queries there instead of typing out the same response yet again. In that post, I explained that, often, the response we get from others is predicated on the way in which we announce our good news. If we are apologetic in our delivery, our mother-in-law may see that as an invitation to lecture us about how much work babies are and how we'd better not expect her to babysit. If we announce our pregnancy sheepishly, our Negative Nelly neighbor may feel free to scoff at how old we will be when our last child finally graduates high school. Willingness to receive children of any number and at any age is quite the revolutionary stance these days, and many view pregnancy announcements as open season for criticism, especially if we seek to defend ourselves against the onslaught with an attitude of embarrassment at the new life growing inside of us.

However, when we announce our "good news of great joy" (Luke 2:10) with the same confidence the angels trumpeted the coming of Jesus—the biggest blessing the world has ever received—who just so happened to arrive in the form of a tiny, helpless, "inconvenient" baby boy, the recipients of our news often feel inspired to "rejoice with those who rejoice" (Romans 12:15).

A Small Act of Defiance

It's no guarantee, of course. There will always be those who insist on putting in their oar of disapproval even when we clearly didn't invite them to help row our boat in the first place. In the ultimate moment of irony, considering it was a post about how to announce pregnancy confidently even in the face of potential backlash, a self-proclaimed Christian woman took the time to leave a detailed comment on my blog explaining the "pull-out method" of birth control so that we would never need to announce a pregnancy again. If you just face-palmed yourself in dismay, sister, I'm with you.

There will always be those who insist on putting in their oar of disapproval even when we clearly didn't invite them to help row our boat in the first place.

The thing is, even when declaring our children the good gifts that they are doesn't inspire a positive response, it can still constitute a small act of defiance against the "god of this world" who "has blinded the minds of those who don't believe" (2 Corinthians 4:4 NLT) and even some who claim they do. After all, it's not just childbearing that has people cringing at the prospect of hard things. It's everything from household chores to exercise programs to marriage building.

I once read (and laughed at) a meme that said, "I keep saying 'Siri' when I mean 'Alexa,' and I just can't believe I live in a world where I can actually mix my robot names up." Of course, twenty years from now, if the Lord hasn't returned and someone stumbles upon this meme, I can only imagine how outdated this sentiment will be. Perhaps we'll be able to think about something and have it materialize at our elbow.

The question, of course, is, would that be a good thing?

I say probably not.

"Quick and Easy" Usually Has Consequences

The human race has had a fascination with growing in knowledge in order to "be like God" (Genesis 3:5) since the Garden of Eden. Sadly, in our desire for "god-likeness" (rather than godliness), our focus remains firmly on ourselves. We strive for expediency and control in the name of "progress," and yet, so often, our obsession with ease is the very thing that keeps us stuck in cycles of self-indulgence and self-sabotage.

TV dinners involve almost no preparation but are laden with preservatives, high levels of sodium, and MSG.

The Bible doesn't mention convenience meals, but 1 Corinthians 10:31 (NIV) does say, "So whether you eat or drink or whatever you do, do it all for the glory of God." Cooking every meal from scratch may not be feasible. But an emphasis on real, unprocessed ingredients over convenience-enhancing chemicals is a way to honor our earthly "temples" (1 Corinthians 6:19), which brings glory to the Lord.

Video games keep kids out of our hair for hours but, when engaged with regularly or in excess, they can lead to addiction, lack of interest in other pursuits, and isolation.

There's nothing in the Bible that outlaws video games (we allow a select few in our home), but Galatians 5:13 declares, "For you were called to freedom, brothers. Only do not use your freedom as an opportunity for the flesh, but through love serve one another." Just because something is allowed does not mean it's beneficial, especially if it becomes an idol for us or our children.

Pacifying with candy ends the tantrum now but sets a worrisome precedent for the future.

The Bible doesn't use the word "tantrum," but Hebrews 12:6 is clear that "the Lord disciplines the one he loves, and chastises every son whom he receives." Forgoing the hard-but-good work of helping our children learn to exercise self-control fails to recognize God's example and standard of care.

An over-the-counter medication might bring a fever down quickly (which is not always a bad thing) but can also mask the illness and have harmful side effects.

The Bible doesn't discuss fever medications (unless you count that time Jesus healed Peter's mother-in-law), but Isaiah 38:21 (NLT) does say, "Make an ointment from figs and spread it over the boil." All right, fine. I just threw that last one in there to see if you were still paying attention.

Christ, Our Example

Clearly, a "quick and easy" mentality often bears negative side effects. What's more, the Bible exhorts us to use Christ as our guide for the way we approach everything, including hard things. And Hebrews 12:2 reminds us that Jesus endured the cross because of the "joy that was set before him." The prospect of honoring and obeying His Father and saving sinners like us from eternal separation and death spurred our Savior on to lay down His very life in a manner that was at once excruciating and humiliating. What a wretched world we'd find ourselves in if Christ had forgone the pain and shame of the cross for the sake of a perfectly understandable preference for the "easy road" (otherwise known as *not death*).

Not only that, but the God-man "learned obedience through what he suffered" (Hebrews 5:8). If hard things are profitable for instruction for even the sinless Savior of the world, how much more so will they benefit us humans who are so bent toward our own sinful way?

We also see Jesus's willingness to put in the hard work of studying God's Word (Luke 2:46), discipling (Luke 6:13), preaching (Matthew 5), and ministering to the sick and hurting (Luke 4:40). He did not simply coast through life on earth, marking time until His sacrificial, saving death, but instead He worked faithfully, even reaching a state of depletion from pouring Himself out for the benefit of others (John 4:6).

We Press On

Imagine an athlete showing up to a decathlon without investing any of the same hard work that his peers had been pouring into their sport for years. Not only would he place dead last, but he would look dead foolish for engaging in a pursuit that so clearly requires dedication and sacrifice.

Or what about a concert pianist who only practices when the fancy strikes her? That's a concert I'll miss, thank you.

Or how about a chess player who never puts in the time to learn proper strategy? She'll be checkmated in no time at all.

We expect a relentless pursuit of excellence from the elite in any arena *because* we know that, without the sacrifice of a daily commitment to their goals, they will never achieve them. We are fine with an expectation of adversity in extreme scenarios. The problem with easy is so obvious when a rigorous training regimen is the deciding factor between a spot on the podium and an "also ran" mention. And yet, in motherhood, a profession that has the potential to guide the everlasting outcome of the souls the Lord has entrusted to us for a time, we often focus solely on the hard things to the exclusion of pressing on "toward the goal for the prize of the upward call of God in Christ Jesus" (Philippians 3:14).

Actually, if we subscribe to the worldly assurance that we deserve a superhero cape simply for holding the title of "mama," we'd probably better avoid Philippians 3 altogether, unless we're looking for a big wallop of conviction. It contains too many phrases like "share his sufferings, becoming like him in his death" and "straining forward to what lies ahead" (verses 10, 13) for us to justify the mantra that simply showing up in motherhood is the equivalent of pursuing it with a dogged commitment to Christ's example.

Will we have hard days? Yes (John 16:33).

Will we fail? Yes! (Philippians 3 acknowledges that too.)

But if we truly believe that we should count whatever worldly satisfaction we may gain by keeping the easy mothering status quo as "loss because of the surpassing worth of knowing Christ Jesus my Lord" (Philippians 3:8), then easy starts to lose its shine a bit. We may look like fools to the world for choosing the harder paths of motherhood. But as Philippians 3:17 (man, it's a good chapter!)

exhorts, when we "keep [our] eyes on those who walk according to the example you have in us" (which is the example of Christ), we receive the "power of his resurrection" (verse 10).

The ultimate problem with easy is that, when we love it, we settle for whatever we can achieve in our own strength in any given moment. The good news about hard is that we never have to do it alone or in our own power. For as Paul points out in Philippians 2:13 (NIV), "It is God who works in you to will and to act in order to fulfill his good purpose."

DAD THOUGHT

As I think back to the days of two helpless-but-demanding kids and how Abbie and I consider that our hardest parenting season, I'm struck by the fact that, on an average day now, we may have:

- A child melting down over a lizard he (literally) loved to death
- Twinbie A sneaking into the bathroom to hide treasures in the porcelain throne
- Twinbie B emptying the dog food into the dog water *again*
- One child practicing piano
- Another child demanding that the piano player "*Stop!*"
- A younger child begging us to play a one-on-one game with him inside
- Yet another asking us to go kick a ball outside
- A middle child needing help on math and reading
- A teen needing more driving practice with us
- Another teen needing relationship advice

Whew! Today's hard objectively makes our "just two" days feel tame by comparison.

So what has changed? Why can we now (mostly) enjoy restaurant dining with rambunctious twins when the same circus-worthy antics from their older siblings led us to swear off eating out for years?

In a word? Experience.

In four words? Skills, perspective, patience, and expectations.

The Lord has used our experiences to enhance our skill set, broaden our perspective, grow our patience, and correct our expectations. We still get frustrated, react poorly, and fail to learn important lessons sometimes, but what used to feel truly daunting or overwhelming just doesn't anymore.

If we never face another challenge in parenting, chances are we'll stagnate. But the proof that we *have* grown is that the things that were difficult ten years ago are now less hard to face. That's something we should strive for and rejoice over.

The Narrative

THE WORLD'S RESPONSE TO HARD	A CHRISTIAN RESPONSE TO HARD
Continually looks for "workarounds" to avoid hard things, regardless of the side effects	Knows that we embrace the hard now for the hope of the good it will bring in the future
Believes the shortest route to ease is the best	Believes that, when necessary, taking the longer, harder road produces perseverance and, in many cases, excellence
Holds that "showing up" is fine because motherhood is hard enough without "trying to be a hero"	Doesn't believe we deserve a standing ovation just for being a mama any more than an athlete deserves a gold medal just for being present at a race

Action Steps

- Memorize and meditate on Romans 12:1-2: "I appeal to you therefore, brothers, by the mercies of God, to present your bodies as a living sacrifice, holy and acceptable to God, which is your spiritual worship. Do not be conformed to this world, but be transformed by the renewal of your mind, that by testing you may discern what is the will of God, what is good and acceptable and perfect."

- Identify one thing you do *because* it's easier (not better), and pray about a game plan to go about it in a more God-honoring way.

- Text your accountability partner at least once this week to let her know your plan and let her know you're praying for her (and then *actually* pray for her!).

Questions

Why, when Scripture makes it so clear that hard things will be part of this earthly life (John 16:33), do I sometimes avoid them at all costs?

What is one motherhood goal I can set for myself that would require me to practically implement the concept "Growth requires struggle"?

What are two easy "sweet spot" aspects of motherhood right now that I can thank God for?

Prayer

Lord, You know our tendency toward escapism, and yet You never escape from us. Thank You that we were "called to freedom" (Galatians 5:13), not as an occasion for indulging our flesh but for serving one another in love. Give us fresh eyes to see the incredible benefit of persevering through hard things.

4

The Hard (but Better) Road of Motherhood

IT WON'T LOOK THE SAME FOR ALL OF US

Right before I sat down to write this chapter, I received a DM from a reader who was clearly a bit miffed about something. She asked me how I could, in all good conscience, claim to have surrendered my fertility to the Lord when I also openly discuss that several of our pregnancies have come at times when we were praying for more space between children or even attempting, through natural family planning (such as abstaining from intimacy during times of peak fertility), to achieve a larger gap. Wasn't I being dishonest? Judgmental? Misleading?

The Struggle to Keep an Open Hand

Setting aside how mightily I had to resist the urge to answer, "Did you actually just ask someone with ten kids if she's really surrendered to the Lord's will for children?" I will say this: She's not wrong *if* I had ever claimed that surrendering my fertility to the Lord meant never struggling with my emotions and desires surrounding the timing of our pregnancies.

Instead, I have always been very clear that my surrender means leaving the ultimate number up to God and then asking Him to help me trust in His will by maintaining an openhanded approach to any "preferences" about timing (preferences that He has repeatedly flouted). Also, I would for sure be peddling a load of malarkey if I had ever claimed it's easy to hold this tension between trust in God for the final number of children and the desire to have a longer break before diving back into pregnancy and the demands of a newborn (or two!).

But I have pretended no such thing.

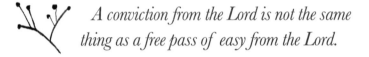 *A conviction from the Lord is not the same thing as a free pass of easy from the Lord.*

In fact, just in case you haven't heard it from me yet, let me say it plainly now: Being openhanded with our fertility is hard. (Let's be honest: Being openhanded with just about any area of our lives is hard.) Do you know why? Because a conviction from the Lord is not the same thing as a free pass of easy from the Lord. (I have so many messages from women who share this conviction and live in the same tension.)

In fact, it's usually the opposite.

Do we feel peace in the knowledge that this is the path the Lord has called us to? Absolutely! But do we also feel the strain of the physical, emotional, and relational demands that each new child places on our family? For sure!

To live is
Christ,
and
to die is gain.

PHILIPPIANS 1:21

Easier but Not Necessarily Better

Many in our ease-obsessed culture would say that feeling the struggle means we have permission (or even the requirement) to abandon our convictions and choose a different path. I have been informed many times how much less complicated my life would be with fewer children. And all it takes to confirm this is the instances when my middle kids are visiting my mom, and we "only" have five kids (three older kids and our twin toddlers) at home. Bedtime feels effortless without the especially rambunctious antics of Theo, Honor, and Shiloh. There are many capable and eager hands to help with the twinbies (our affectionate term for our twin boys), and the house is eerily quiet in comparison to its usual weekday hubbub.

It's a nice break, honestly.

But is it better?

I think of Jesus sweating actual drops of blood in the Garden of Gethsemane and asking the Father to take the cup of anguish from His lips (Luke 22:44).

I think of Paul declaring, "For to me to live is Christ, and to die is gain" (Philippians 1:21).

I think of Jim Elliot famously asserting, "He is no fool who gives what he cannot keep to gain that which he cannot lose" before giving up his very life at the point of an Auca spear.

I think of Corrie ten Boom's struggle to forgive the Nazis who killed so many of her family members.

Wouldn't their lives have been better if they had simply chosen an easier path? Cut corners? Left the really dirty work to someone else?

It depends on your definition of "better." If by "better" we mean safer, more convenient, and less demanding, then perhaps.

But Corrie ten Boom didn't think so. To her, "There is no safer place than in the center of the will of God."

A Life of True Surrender

After working with the Dutch underground to help almost 800 Jews escape the Nazis, she was captured by the Gestapo and carted off to a concentration camp (where her beloved sister, Betsie, perished). If you know nothing else of her life, that should help you understand that her definition of "safe" was very different from most people's. Would it have been safer for her Christian father, Casper, to have forgone wearing a yellow star to identify with the suffering of his Jewish neighbors? Physically, yes. But not spiritually, according to an old man so frail in body that he died almost immediately after being imprisoned for his acts of defiance.

Still, his certainty in the rightness of his surrender to God's will was never shaken. In a moving account, his grandson, Peter, describes the elder ten Boom's determination, following their arrest, to buoy the spirits of his family members by reading from Psalm 91 as they were held prisoner in a gymnasium, awaiting a grim fate. Despite his grandfather's assurances, doubt filled Peter's heart at their circumstances:

> Tragedy had struck. Where was the host of angels we had prayed for so often? Had God forgotten us? Then I glanced over at Grandfather sitting in the corner. There was such an expression of peace on his pale face that I could not help marveling. He actually was protected. God had built a fence around him.
>
> At last they took me to my cell. As I walked past Grandfather, I stopped, bent over him, and kissed him goodbye. He looked up at me and said, "My boy, are we not a privileged generation?"

If you just choked back a sob at such courageous composure, you are not alone. What an exquisite testimony to the joy and confidence that come from persisting in the spiritual safety of the center of God's oh-so-gracious and dangerously countercultural will for our lives.

So what does this have to do with us as mothers?

So much, sweet sisters!

For Love of Our Children and Obedience to God

Just ask my friend Taylor, who is bravely mothering four little siblings, whom she and her husband adopted from foster care, while their baby sister faces an uncertain future. Her unconventional road to motherhood includes multiple miscarriages and a tragic accident that rendered her body unlikely to ever sustain a pregnancy. Hers is a hard I can only imagine but one that inspires me to say with Job, "Though he slay me, yet will I hope in him," for "he knows the way that I take; when he has tested me, I will come forth as gold" (Job 13:15; 23:10 NIV).

You see, if you thought I was trying to equate having ten kids with the only way to walk the hard-but-good narrow road in motherhood, you couldn't be more wrong.

For starters, having ten kids is not God's will for many women (and I say this having heard from dozens of women who have never taken any form of birth control and still have far fewer than ten children), and my particular challenges as a mama of many are not some sort of A-level achievement in comparison to any other. In fact, when I consider the legal hoops Taylor has had to jump through in order to welcome her children home, pregnancy and childbirth seem refreshingly straightforward.

Is my friend being dishonest when she says that adoption is beautiful? That motherhood is a gift? That she is surrendered to the Lord's will in fostering, even on the days when anxiety over her children's missing their baby sister steals her sleep and rings her eyes black with exhaustion?

No!

This sweet mama is proclaiming with her actions the profound sacrifice of one of the foundational truths of Christianity we take for granted—God's adoption of us as His children (Romans 8:15; 9:26; Galatians 3:26)—and it is excruciatingly inspiring to witness her willingness to endure the unknown, the trauma, the drudgery of complicated forms and court dates and home visits and intrusive questions and unjust bereavement, all for love of her children and obedience to God.

I am likewise heartened by the perseverance of my best friend and business partner, Lindsay (who does the incredible artwork in my books). With three children, she has maintained an openness to more—a willingness the Lord has answered with almost a decade of secondary infertility. Her oldest daughter, Evie, is on the autism spectrum, and "hard" barely begins to describe the daily litany of therapies, medications, coping mechanisms, and appointments Lindsay must navigate in order to be the best God-ordained mom for her precious girl. Having had the privilege of witnessing my best friend's struggle firsthand, I can say, without a doubt, that the Lord has made her both more resilient and more malleable as a result of it. Her hard looks nothing like mine. But I love her all the more because I have witnessed it. And I love God all the more for sustaining her through it.

It's Not a Contest

Maybe your mothering hard is a completely different "flavor" from the ones I've already mentioned.

A chronically ill child.

An unbelieving, unsupportive spouse.

Single parenting.

An all-consuming full-time job you can't quit.

Toxic, antagonistic relatives.

_____.

(Feel free to insert your own challenge in the blank.)

Maybe your struggle is the one the world finds the hardest to comprehend: the willing relinquishment of your own freedoms and the "squandering" of your money-earning potential for the sake of being the primary discipler, caregiver, and love-tank filler for your children.

Maybe the constant bottom wiping, spill cleaning, boo-boo kissing, story reading, crumb sweeping, fight refereeing, and tantrum soothing feel inconsequential compared to some of the scenarios I listed above, and yet you still find yourself floundering in the deep end of mundane motherhood, wondering how repeating the same seven actions every single day can feel quite so ridiculously hard.

Maybe you're questioning yet again why you're "just" a stay-at-home mom when you have an engineering or teaching degree, have passed the CPA exam, or have a talent you're not using in a way the world deems legitimate.

Maybe you think that if one more "well-meaning" woman at the grocery store tells you you're wasting your time homeschooling your kids and how maladjusted they'll be if you continue, you'll enroll them in the next public school you drive by.

The Ultimate Example of Hard

Every single one of these scenarios (and so many more) has the potential to rattle the courage and shake the confidence of those who rebel against the culture of mediocre motherhood with its assurances of the ease and comfort and "me time" we "deserve."

And so we return to the burning question of this chapter: "I know if I simply quit _____ (pick the hard that applies to you), my life would be easier. But *would that be better?*"

Or are we, as Casper ten Boom so boldly proclaimed, *privileged* to be part of the generation who is ridiculed for the "foolishness" of choosing the steep road in motherhood?

We have only to look at one example—that of Jesus—to discover the answer.

Because He prayed, "Not my will, but yours be done" (Luke 22:42) and meant it, we have the gift of salvation and eternal life with Him. Because of His openhanded approach to ultimate suffering, we can be called sons and daughters of God. Because He recognized that easier, in this case, was not in fact better, we have a hope that "does not disappoint, because the love of God has been poured out within our hearts through the Holy Spirit who was given to us" (Romans 5:5 NASB).

Because of Jesus's openhanded approach to ultimate suffering, we can be called sons and daughters of God.

Don't expect to look around at the paragons of motherhood in worldly culture and recognize yourself if you have committed to living in the tension of surrendering to the Lord's will and battling a fleshly desire for the easy road.

Don't even expect to recognize yourself in every struggle that a fellow Christian mama endures. There is common ground, yes, and thank God for that! But the Bible gives us no assurance that we will find a perfect parallel to our own circumstances. We are all uniquely created by Him, with no duplicates! We are only assured that "as we share abundantly in Christ's sufferings, so through Christ we share abundantly in comfort too" (2 Corinthians 1:5). And thank God for that as well!

As we share abundantly in Christ's sufferings, so through Christ we share abundantly in comfort too.

Do expect to be misunderstood, mocked, marginalized, and dismissed by a society that cannot comprehend the value of forgoing ease with the view that I stressed earlier: "This light momentary affliction is preparing for us an eternal weight of glory beyond all comparison" (2 Corinthians 4:17). For we know "the message of the cross is foolishness to those who are perishing, but to us who are being saved it is the power of God" (1 Corinthians 1:18 NIV). It's truly the only form of "empowerment" that will ever do the Christian mama any good.

Choosing the hard but better road in motherhood (*whatever* that looks like for each of us specifically) in that power mandates a daily, sometimes hourly, commitment to look to Jesus (rather than social media or alcohol or peer validation or any other crutch) as our hope—our "anchor for the soul, firm and secure" (Hebrews 6:19 NIV). But it is a choice worth making again and again. We can say with Corrie ten Boom that trusting Christ is the only "safe" option and with her nephew, Peter, "The everlasting arms are around all of us. God does not make mistakes. He is at the controls."

DAD THOUGHT

Just as your hard will not always look like your neighbor's, your hard will not always look like your husband's either.

In our polarized culture, we are often told we are *supposed* to choose between these two options:

1. Completely dismantle the concept of gender roles in marriage and split everything fifty-fifty. "I work a day job, you work a day job. I change a diaper, you change a diaper. I get up at night, you get up at night. I get an hour of free time, you get an hour of free time."

2. Legalistically adhere to traditional arrangements of a male breadwinner and a female housewife. "Dad better stay out of the kitchen while Mom keeps her hands off the finances. Or Mom changes the diapers while Dad changes the oil."

The first example ignores God's design for marriage, and the second elevates traditional gender roles to Ten Commandment–level status. Both miss the Bible's emphasis on following Christ's example of servant-heartedness and humility in favor of rigid rules. Galatians 6:2-5 helps shed some light on the truth:

> *Bear one another's burdens*, and so fulfill the law of Christ. For if anyone thinks he is something, when he is nothing, he deceives himself. But let each one test his own work, and then his reason to boast will be in himself alone and not in his neighbor. *For each will have to bear his own load.*

We each have our own loads of primary responsibility to bear, and in the breakdown of household duties, I believe our primary roles should reflect our God-given talents, preferences, and circumstances first. In more cases than not, the result will mirror a traditional male-female dynamic because God has gifted men and women with unique temperaments and strengths that naturally lend themselves to particular tasks. It is far from a universal rule though. Regardless of who "runs point" for any given job, God's Word calls us to share in the work and support our spouses rather than focus on our burdens alone.

And did you catch the bonus exhortation Paul places in the middle there—"Test his own work"?

We must remember not to compare our load to our neighbor's load or the efforts of our spouse to the efforts of our neighbor's spouse. We are called to bear and to share but not to compare.

If it sounds like I've veered off the parenting path into marriage territory, it's important to remember that we are modeling for our children how to share and work together. This is a critical lesson for our children, one that will bear fruit in their relationships with us, their siblings, and their spouses-to-be, ultimately creating households of greater peace, both now and in the future.

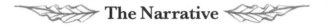 **The Narrative**

THE WORLD'S RESPONSE TO HARD	A CHRISTIAN RESPONSE TO HARD
Keeps an eye out for other people's "hards" to compare	Strives to keep all eyes on Jesus, the author and finisher of our faith
Resents all perceived unfairness, including being "bullied" by our children	Counts it a privilege to endure hardship for Christ, *including* that of our children's more difficult behavior
Ridicules those who choose a harder road, often from a place of feeling "called out"	Cheers fellow mamas on in their pursuit of Christlike excellence

 **Action Steps**

- Memorize and meditate on Philippians 1:21: "For to me to live is Christ, and to die is gain."
- Write down one area in which the Lord is calling you to choose the "hard but better" road in motherhood. (Your family's health? Personal time with the Lord? Schooling choices?)
- Touch base with your accountability partner and commit to praying over these areas of conviction this week.

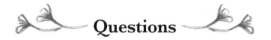 **Questions**

How do I respond when friends, family, or strangers mock me for pursuing a path of "unnecessary hardship" (in their eyes)?

Is my response biblical? Why or why not?

In what ways am I *privileged* to endure hardship for the sake of Christ and my family's growth?

Prayer

Lord, we know that You chose the hard road of the cross for our sakes, and yet we so often want to coast in Your grace, rather than pressing "on toward the goal for the prize of the upward call of God in Christ Jesus" (Philippians 3:14). Help us to freely embrace Your example of following the hard, but better, road in motherhood.

5

Fear Is a Liar

WE CAN DO MORE HARD THINGS THAN WE THINK WE CAN

If you read that last chapter and felt a combination of "pumped up and raring to tackle hard things" and "scared spitless," I don't blame you. I have felt that way often. Still do sometimes, if I'm honest.

I can read missionary story after missionary story and feel both inspired and a little bit worried about what the logistics would look like if God were to call me to reach remote people groups in Africa with the gospel like He did Mary Slessor or to ask me to mother my children alone for His glory like He did Elisabeth Elliot.

Would Jesus Be Enough?

While the Africa option feels like a bit of a stretch for our family (I'm not saying He won't do it!), the prospect of widowhood has loomed in my mind at times, especially with a husband who travels often. I distinctly remember a time when Shaun was on a work trip, and I hadn't heard from him all day. That, in itself, wasn't cause for worry. He usually calls to say good morning, but when he is working from a different time zone or has an especially busy or early start to his day, I won't hear from him until evening. But I can count on one hand the number of times I haven't received a phone call before 10:00 p.m. So when 10:15 p.m. rolled around with no contact, I tried to call him.

After my calls went straight to voice mail three times in a row, I sent a text. When that produced no response, I shot him a quick email to see if his phone was malfunctioning (are you chuckling with me over the variety of electronic methods for spouse monitoring we have at our disposal these days?). I'd have sent a carrier pigeon too if I'd felt like it would do any good.

After an hour of no reply, genuine concern began to sit uncomfortably, like an undigested meal, beneath my ribs. The story of a reader skittered through my mind—a sweet mama of seven young children whose husband had suffered a fatal stroke while driving. What if Shaun were lying unconscious in a ditch, out of cell phone range, his life's blood slowly seeping from his veins? It sounds macabre, but it's not outside the realm of reasonable possibility. I don't love it when he travels for work, but I also don't hate it because we have our routines, and we know he'll be home soon. But what if "soon" never came again?

Could I gracefully handle such loss? How would I be all the things that my children need from both me and Shaun? What would shouldering the burden of the financial load he carries look like? Would the Lord sustain me? Could I still praise His name through my grief?

I'm not even particularly prone to worry, and yet I found myself battling the nonsensical urge to call everyone we knew to see if anyone could somehow get through to my husband when I could not.

Thankfully, this particular story has a very happy ending. I hadn't been able to reach Shaun because his phone was in airplane mode as he winged his way home—surprise!—a full day earlier than we had anticipated.

Phew, right?

Still, as the story of the ten Booms clearly illustrates, even when we find ourselves in the very center of God's will, a tragedy-free life is never our due. In fact,

Jesus banishes any doubt with these words: "In this world you will have trouble" (John 16:33 NIV).

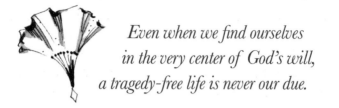

*Even when we find ourselves
in the very center of God's will,
a tragedy-free life is never our due.*

Heroes of the Faith

So how do we fight back the panic that threatens to cripple our nerve when we contemplate the frailty of this life? How do we ever do anything hard or courageous or bold (all of which ramp up our risk factors considerably) when, for example, simply strapping ourselves into the death machines, er, vehicles we drive each day results in 1.35 million deaths worldwide every year?

The answer, quite simply, is to live by faith.

Oh, nice one, Abbie. Way to pull out the clichés. Are you going to give me a poster with a kitten dangling by her claws from a tree limb and tell me to "hang in there" too?

Now, hear me out, friends. I think "faith" has gotten a bad rap, thanks to the overabundance of references to it in vaguely "spiritual" movies, song lyrics, and, yes, inspirational cat posters.

However, when we unpack the biblical definition of the word, faith looks far from trite (and often veers into downright audacious territory). Hebrews 11:1-3 explains that "faith is the assurance of things hoped for, the conviction of things not seen. For by it the people of old received their commendation. By faith we understand that the universe was created by the word of God, so that what is seen was not made out of things that are visible."

Words like "assurance" and "conviction" hardly have a namby-pamby ring. And when we look at the examples of faith in action in the rest of Hebrews 11, we see why. By faith, Abraham left everything for an unknown country, believing God would bring a nation as densely populated as the sands of the seashore from his old, tired, childless loins (verses 8-12). By faith, Moses trusted God would do the impossible and free the Israelites from enslavement to an Egyptian tyrant (verses 23-29). The chapter goes on to detail the miracles God performed through the conviction and assurance he had given Joshua, Gideon, Rahab, Sarah, Samson, David, Solomon—everyday human beings like you and me. Never does the faith of Hebrews 11 sound even a little bit nebulous or ineffectual. Instead, it is electric, contagious even!

More Than a Bumper Sticker

Speaking of Joshua, chances are you've seen the famous "be strong and courageous" verse plastered on a T-shirt, bumper sticker, or coffee mug a time or two. Not surprising when we remember that between verses 6 and 9 of Joshua chapter 1, the Lord tells Joshua to "be strong and courageous" not once, not twice, but three times in a row. He even throws a "do not be frightened, and do not be dismayed" (verse 9) in there for an extra kick in the pants.

For the sake of context, Moses, the great prophet-leader of Israel, has just died, and the mantle of power and responsibility has shifted to Joshua's shoulders. I think that promotion alone might warrant at least two "strong and courageous" pep talks. But Joshua is not simply keeping the Mosaic status quo. Instead, he has been tasked with marching into the Promised Land to claim the territories the Lord promised the Israelites decades before. War is looming. And Joshua has over "600,000 fighting men" to wrangle into action and order.

Talk about intense pressure and totally justifiable "frightened and dismayed" responses!

But no. The Lord straight up tells Joshua not to go there. Instead, He assures him that it won't even be trusty Josh doing the fighting. As Joshua 1:13 (NIV) says, "The LORD your God will give you rest by giving you this land." And then the Lord does exactly what He says when the Israelites defeat the fortified city of Jericho, not with epic feats of masculinity and warcraft but with a simple march around and around the city walls, tooting their own horns (ha) and hollering (as we Southerners call it) a lot. (You can read about this in Joshua 6.)

BE STRONG AND COURAGEOUS.

JOSHUA 1:9

Trust and Obey, for There's No Other Way

Even when God has given us detailed instructions, how often do we find ourselves hesitant to step out in faith—especially if they're instructions we don't like?

If the Lord tells me to go talk to that new mama and give her some encouragement, and then the perfect words just pop into my brain, I'm liable to hop right over and introduce myself. But what if all I have is a strong impression that I'm supposed to reach out and then a much vaguer "I'll give you the words to say once you get there"?

Or what if what He wants us to do makes absolutely no sense? Wait—I'm supposed to invite that former friend, the one who rejected me in no uncertain terms, to lunch without knowing how she'll respond or what in the world we'll talk about once we're sitting there staring at each other awkwardly? *No thanks, Lord.* And yet the Lord asked me to obey Him in these exact circumstances several years ago, and then, when I did, He blessed the encounter with peace.

My DMs are full of messages like these:

"I would love more kids, but I'm scared of how I will manage because my two-year-old is a handful already."

"I feel like I'm being called to homeschool, but I'm worried I won't know how to handle multiple levels at once."

"We feel this pull toward adoption, but I'm nervous because I don't know if I'm equipped for all the trauma that comes with it."

"I think the Lord wants me to pursue reconciliation with this contentious family member, but being vulnerable feels really scary."

Listen, friends: If you ever feel like you're the only one who freaks out a little (or a lot) when God asks you to do hard stuff, may I refer you to the above "heroes of faith" from Hebrews 11? They're not cartoon action figures but real, actual human beings with genuine emotions and insecurities just like yours and mine.

The Lord Is Patient and Slow to Anger

When the Lord speaks directly to Moses, Moses still drags his feet (multiple times!). In Exodus 3, from verses 12-22, God lays out *exactly* what the process of emancipating the Israelites from Pharaoh will look like. He even gives Moses a script and assures him of a favorable outcome. And still Moses waffles. Okay, fine, he pretty much acts like a stubborn mule.

Here is just a smattering of his objections (I'm paraphrasing, but you can find the exact conversation in Exodus 4:1-17):

"What if they do not believe me or listen to me?"

"Pardon your servant, Lord. I have never been eloquent...I am slow of speech and tongue."

And then, in his most on-the-nose version of "Yeah, no," he says, "Pardon your servant, Lord. Please send someone else."

At this point, God's wrath burns against Moses, and I don't blame Him one bit. It's easy to feel frustrated with Moses's first objection, considering that God had told him in the previous chapter what to do if the Israelites tried to "call his bluff" (which was no bluff at all). But instead of striking Moses dead on the spot for being obstinate, the Lord says, "What about your big brother, Aaron? He speaks well. You'll tell him what to say, and then he'll say it. I'll be with you every step of the way."

And yet, despite our annoyance at Moses's hesitance in the face of direct revelation from the *God of the universe*, we'll admit, if we're honest, that it's much easier to watch a gunfight on TV and wonder why it took the hero so long to pull his gun than it is to strap on our own holsters and stride out into the dusty streets for a showdown.

We Still Don't Get a Free Pass

I love that God—in spite of His understandable anger—accommodates Moses's backpedaling response by providing him with a way (smooth-talking Aaron) to feel more confident. Notice God still doesn't let Moses off the hook though. In Exodus 4:17 (NIV), God tells him, "But take this staff in your hand so you can perform the signs with it." In other words, "I'll make it easier on you, but *you're still going!*"

A quick glance at Gideon's story (he's the guy who receives an angelic visitation while threshing his wheat in secret so the Midianite bullies don't steal his dinner—Judges 6:11), Sarah's account (she's the gal who laughed when God told her she would bear a child in her old age—Genesis 18:12), or David's journey (Ever read the Psalms? His pleas for help and comfort make great ready-made prayers!) reveals similar examples of ordinary men and women who received some pretty extraordinary callings.

The Lord accomplished His purposes (saving the Israelites from their oppressors, opening the barren womb, establishing a king after His own heart) through their faltering, flawed obedience. And the good news is He's just as mighty and faithful to do the same through you and me now.

Death to the Comfort Zone

So to each of the concerned mamas I mentioned earlier, I say this: Yes, it might be incredibly tough in certain seasons. You might be driven beyond your human capacity for patience and resourcefulness right into the arms of a God who loves you enough to refuse to allow you to stay in your comfort zone, unchallenged and unchanged—who adores you enough to give you the kind of hard that transforms you from someone who wishes she could live for Him into someone who's doing it right now, even while she doubts her capacity to do it again tomorrow.

You might be driven beyond your human capacity for patience and resourcefulness right into the arms of a God who loves you enough to refuse to allow you to stay in your comfort zone, unchallenged and unchanged—who adores you enough to give you the kind of hard that transforms you from someone who wishes she could live for Him into someone who's doing it right now, even while she doubts her capacity to do it again tomorrow.

If you're reading these words and still feeling that tingle of fear, let me remind you that, while our emotions are real, while they're effective tools for connection and encouragement, they are also often unreliable barometers for truth. Fear, especially, is a mythomaniac (that's just fancy speak for "chronic liar," but isn't it a fantastic word?). Fear's knee-jerk response to just about anything is "I could never…" But very rarely is this true, even from a purely secular perspective.

"I could never skydive." Actually, while it might terrify them, most people are physically capable of strapping on a parachute and jumping out of an airplane.

"I could never learn to play an instrument well." Believe it or not, research shows that repetition and committed practice serve a much larger role in the mastery of a skill than natural propensity ever could.

"I could never run my own company." Honestly, even the most intimidated types find themselves capable of success once they've pushed past that initial belief that "these kinds of things just magically happen to other people."

I'm living proof of this. I spent years scared of the time commitment it would take to get a book published, scared of the amount of research it would take to do it well, scared of rejection, scared of the responsibility of marketing it to a readership, scared of not having anything worthwhile to add to the conversation. My own mother once told me, when I was fretting about how I would find time to write with small children and so many responsibilities, "You don't have to be the one to say it. Somebody else will come along to write it if it needs to be said." She meant it as an encouragement to alleviate the pressure of adding another thing to my plate, but it felt like a confirmation of that last insecurity I mentioned: My voice wasn't necessary.

Doing It Afraid

And yet, all the while, I kept blogging and posting to social media and praying the Lord would multiply my efforts. I showed up day after day doing what felt feasible with the pockets of time I had, asking the Lord to help me be content with the reach and the kind of writing He had given in that moment. I hardly dared to entertain the thought that the very thing I feared and hoped for most might come to pass, because the gap between "blogging" and "published" felt too big for this busy mama of many to bridge.

And then, one ho-hum day, as I put my baby down for a nap and hustled to get the laundry and dishes done before he woke up, the Lord took the very scenario that "only happens to other people"—namely, a publisher approaching me with a book deal—and used it to show me that, as Elisabeth Elliot puts it, "Sometimes when we are called to obey, the fear does not subside and we are expected to move against the fear. One must choose to do it afraid."

If I'd allowed my fear of everything that comes along with being a "real writer" to keep me from writing at all, I wouldn't be here, pecking away at my second book in a coffee shop, right now. My debut effort, *M Is for Mama*, would never have become a bestselling book. And my mom would never have come to me and said, "The world needs your voice, Abbie. You have written something that honors God." I thank God with a smile, whenever I think of the moment I first saw my publisher's email in my inbox, that He didn't give me the whole picture from the beginning. That, instead, He continually pushed me a little further beyond what I thought I was capable of in my own strength. That He made it so obvious that it was He, not I, who had accomplished His purpose of making me a published author in His timing and His way.

I could give you so many other examples of things God has been gracious enough to make me do scared, some of which I'll share later in the book, but for now, I'll just encourage you with the instructions the Lord gave Joshua as He called him to do what should have been not only scary but downright impossible: "This Book of the Law shall not depart from your mouth, but you shall meditate on it day and night, so that you may be careful to do according to all that is written in it. For then you will make your way prosperous, and then you will have good success" (Joshua 1:8).

A Different Kind of Prosperity

Notice this "prosperity formula" says nothing about "believing in yourself," "following your heart," "being a boss babe," "manifesting," "naming it and claiming it," or any other kind of inspiring-sounding but ultimately empty drivel the world hoses us down with on the daily. Instead, it assures Joshua that the road to success (in a biblical sense) is found not within his own abilities or strengths but in a daily meditation on and adherence to Scripture and God's ways of doing things, which results in a resolve that "as for me and my house, we will serve the Lord" (Joshua 24:15).

How refreshingly countercultural and, ultimately, freeing (versus "hustle culture," which is a prison of our own making). We might stare, dry-mouthed and weak-kneed, at the seemingly insurmountable tasks the Lord places like big ol' boulders of faith in our path. That's okay. Because we don't have to accomplish them alone. The Lord literally tells Moses, "I will be with you" (Exodus 3:12), and Moses still tries to get out of it. I bet you can relate (I know I can). Here's the truth, though: We are capable of doing way harder things than we give ourselves credit for, not because we deserve more credit but because God does.

He only asks that we inch forward in faith and watch Him do exactly what He said He will while He gets all the glory He deserves.

He only asks that we inch forward in faith and watch Him do exactly what He said He will while He gets all the glory He deserves.

DAD THOUGHT

Though you might have guessed from my comments on the last chapter that I don't believe the father should be the family's cruise *director*, always dictating "what, when, and how," I do believe the father should most often be the family's cruise *control*.

By that I mean he should be the one watching out for whether the family is doing too little and stagnating or doing too much and risking burnout.

As fathers, we have a God-given desire to defend and protect the family. We are on the lookout for threats, whether they come from without or within. This protective concern serves as a brake, causing us to weigh the pros and cons and say no when we're taking on too much or when our lives are unavoidably full.

However, we can also allow that fear to cause us to hesitate when God is saying "go" or "do." Worse yet, we can start to conflate laziness with wisdom in an attempt to justify taking it easy on ourselves, and end up comfortably coasting.

But coasting is not our calling.

Our calling is to "run with perseverance the race marked out for us" (Hebrews 12:1 NIV), not to sit on the couch with a bowl of chips while we watch someone else compete. As participants, we should run with purpose in order to complete the race as well as we are able. That requires both knowing our limits and pushing ourselves to expand them.

Fathers should be looking to find a balance of activity that protects the family but also drives spiritual growth and reliance on God.

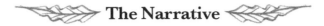

The Narrative

THE WORLD'S RESPONSE TO HARD	A CHRISTIAN RESPONSE TO HARD
Feels afraid of hard things	Knows that God has not given us a spirit of fear
Tries to get out of unpleasant tasks	Says, "Not my will but Yours be done, Lord, even if I don't like it"
Equates fear with truth	Acknowledges that fear is a liar

Action Steps

- Memorize and meditate on Hebrews 11:1-3: "Faith is the assurance of things hoped for, the conviction of things not seen. For by it the people of old received their commendation. By faith we understand that the universe was created by the word of God, so that what is seen was not made out of things that are visible."

- Identify and write down two motherhood areas that cause you consistent worry.

- Choose one area to pray for specifically once a day this week with an attitude of "Thy will be done, Lord."

Questions

What has the Lord called you to that you're afraid of right now?

In obeying Him, what is the worst thing that could happen? What's the best?

How has God shown Himself faithful in the past during challenging times?

Prayer

Lord, You have not given us a spirit of fear but of "power and love and self-control" (2 Timothy 1:7). Thank You for never leaving us or forsaking us. May we continue to recognize Your faithfulness to us as we take tiny steps of faith to obey You in the little things, the hard things, and the scary things.

6

Gluttons for Punishment

WHEN THE HARD IS ACTUALLY OUR FAULT

Shaun and I have built two DIY homes together from scratch—once in our twenties when we had two small children and once in our thirties when we had seven (still relatively) small children. I add "from scratch" to the DIY part because, no matter how many times I say this, people incredulously ask, "Do you really mean that you did practically all of it, not just the general contracting, yourself?"

Yep. By the grace of God, we actually did.

And even after having done it twice, I still sometimes gaze in awe at a wall in our home and think, "My husband built every bit of that and the one it's attached to, wired the electricity for the lights and power outlets, and even ran the plumbing for the bathroom right behind that wall." *Whoa.*

Eating the Elephant

Both builds were incredibly daunting undertakings that we accomplished in classic "how do you eat an elephant" fashion: by planning every painstaking detail for months, then tackling one task at a time, over and over again, until they were all finally done. Well, most of them, anyway. I say "most" because there is a syndrome among hardcore renovators and DIY homebuilders that I will call "building fatigue" (I've had this confirmed by numerous acquaintances who've built their own homes as well). After pushing so hard to get everything "dried in" against the weather, then move-in ready, then more or less furnished and decorated, you're so sick of hammers and home improvement stores that you swear off doing anything related to construction or décor for the next decade.

Did Shaun single-handedly install every bit of the siding on our current home? Yep. (It took him three full months of weekends!)

Was our master bathtub for which I accidentally bought the wrong faucet nonfunctioning for over five years after we moved in? Yes to that too, although it's working now! (The consolation prize: Showering together under the double showerheads we installed has become one of our favorite things.)

Did I wallpaper the stairwell with the twenty-foot drop that I couldn't get even the professionals to look at twice? Yep.

Did I ever go back and wallpaper that one corner in the bathroom that was too high to reach without an extension ladder? Yes, but it took me four years and a deadline of people coming to stay in our home.

Another building fatigue casualty? Our awesomely chippy seafoam-green vintage pantry door. It was everything my funky-door-loving self could have dreamed of, minus a doorknob. And it remained knob-less throughout four of our children's toddlerhoods, resulting in more gleeful cereal-dumping sprees, more paper napkin massacres, and more tender feet rescued from shards of broken mason jars than I care to admit.

The Architects of Our Own Misery

Finally, one day, Shaun spotted me emerging from the pantry with the twinbies—in football holds, one under each arm. He noticed my weary expression and did a U-turn for his workshop. Five minutes later, we had a pantry door-knob, and I was able to spend the time I had been devoting to guarding the entrance (like a goalie in sudden death overtime) instead on contemplating *why* in the name of angel hair pasta and pretzel sticks it had taken us so long to implement such a simple fix to such an irksome problem.

The clear juxtaposition between the ease of the solution and the magnitude of the frustration highlights just how capable we are of being the architects of our own misery, even in mundane ways. Clearly, the hard things we experience are not always the result of circumstances beyond our control but can arise from our own laziness, neglect, pride, or even willful sins of selfishness and greed.

 *Clearly, the hard things we experience are not always the result of circumstances beyond our control but can arise from our own laziness, neglect, pride, or even willful sins of selfishness and greed.*

Sometimes we invite trouble through the door simply by our unchecked ambition of "supermom-dom."

One year, I decided it would be a good idea to stack my Monday so deep that my nose was barely above water by the end of the day:

- Wake up at 4:45 a.m. to teach an early morning fitness class? *Check.*
- Rush home to get seven kids ready for homeschool co-op? *Check.*
- Spend all day at co-op teaching two sections of high school Spanish and feverishly grading so I don't have any work to take home with me? *Check.*
- Round the kids up from co-op, then drop off several at piano practice? *Check.*

- Take the rest of the kids to the grocery store? *Check.*
- Pick up piano kids, then drop off different kids at dance? *Check.*
- Run more errands during dance practice? *Check.*
- Take all the kids home and start dinner the moment I walk in the door? *Check.*
- Clean up after dinner and tackle the laundry? *Check.*
- Get all the kids in bed? *Check.*
- Collapse in exhaustion? *Double check.*

Oh, and did I mention I was either pregnant with Shiloh or freshly postpartum and breastfeeding during this entire school year? Honestly, it was over-the-top too much, but I was too stubborn to admit it. I told myself if I could muscle through the hard of one overstuffed day for one year, we would all be the better for it.

I was wrong.

When We're Far from Fine

The self-imposed stress of that one day trickled over into other areas of my life, until Shaun finally asked me, one Sunday afternoon in the spring, if everything was okay. I remember whipping my head up to glare at him, feeling unreasonably peevish at the question.

"Yes. Everything's FINE." (*Obviously.*)

He raised his eyebrows mildly and let it go, but the Holy Spirit prodded my heart to apologize that evening as I loaded the washing machine, feeling panicked over a vague nagging sensation that felt like a slippery fish I couldn't seem to grasp. Why was I so irritable? *Was* I okay? Why did my chest feel so tight? Sundays used to be my favorite day of the week, but as I mulled over my snappish reaction to Shaun's question, it occurred to me that I'd been feeling anxious and jittery beginning around 4:30 p.m. every single Sunday afternoon for weeks. As the rest of my family relaxed together during the evening, I would wipe down the table and rearrange things, unable to find a place to land, subconsciously dreading Monday.

What was wrong?

It took more time, prayer, and a Holy Spirit–inspired round of something I named the Gentleness Challenge (see page 89) before I could think clearly enough to recognize that the demands of a newborn plus wonky postpartum hormones plus manic Mondays (not to mention homeschooling and regular life for the remainder of the week) do not make for restful Sabbath Sundays. And they don't make for a particularly nice mama the rest of the week either.

Of course, all these stresses spilled over into my family's lives and attitudes as well. The phrase "If Mama ain't happy, ain't nobody happy" is all too often wielded as an excuse for self-focus. After all, if Mama doesn't get her coffee-time, me-time, show-time, wine-time, girlfriend-time, then she deserves not to be happy. And if Mama ain't happy, ain't nobody else *gonna be happy*. It is an ultimatum to keep the matriarch of the house chipper and cheerful, *or else*.

We Set the Tone

But another angle of the sentiment is heart-prickingly true: When we're struggling with stress and our body language and words reflect this conflict, our kids and our husband will often begin to mimic our snippy tones, which results in a whole lot of nervous, cranky people under one roof. After all, Proverbs 25:24 says, "It is better to live in a corner of the housetop than in a house shared with a quarrelsome wife."

Some will interpret this as a slam on all women, but I believe it is, instead, an acknowledgment of the immense sway we hold over the atmosphere of our homes. We bear the weighty privilege of being our household's emotional thermostat—a responsibility that feels all the heavier when we face times of increased pressure or hormonal imbalance. Or both, in my case. So many of these challenges come whether we invite them or not, which is why it's so important to choose our yeses carefully so we have some margin for grace when the struggles inevitably arrive.

I had promised myself that committing to so many things on the first workday of the week would set me up for less busyness the other six days. And while that might have been true, the benefit did little to mitigate the unnecessary toll it took on my depleted, pregnant (and later, postpartum) self. It only took a tiny bit of honesty to admit that we would all have been better off switching piano and dance to a different day.

Also? Grocery pickup is life changing.

 *Grocery pickup is life changing.*

A Common Ailment

Chances are you're nodding along in commiseration, wincing as you remember that time you committed to heading up VBS while also taking your four-year-old to speech therapy four days a week and hosting that foreign exchange student for the last two weeks of summer. Turns out, making our own lives harder than necessary is a common motherhood ailment. Just ask the thousands of women who responded with gusto in just a few short hours to a query about the ways we make things complicated for ourselves.

Not surprisingly, the number one item that soared far above any other on the list of self-inflicted hard things is staying up too late when we know we should go to bed—*especially* in light of the fact that toddlers will always wake up at 5:46 a.m. with zero consideration for our "need" to unwind with another episode of *Gilmore Girls* while folding a basket of laundry at 1:00 a.m.

We push past a reasonable bedtime with burning, gritty eyes, crafting earrings for our Etsy shop or getting lost in a novel. Or writing a chapter in a motherhood book, perhaps? *Ahem.* We tell ourselves it's "worth it" because, for many of us, it's the only uninterrupted time we've had all day. And yet, inevitably, when we wake up with a splitting headache to a six-year-old mouth-breathing in our face and discover that the baby has divested himself of his diaper and painted a poop mural on the wall *again*, we can't help but question how worthwhile it really is to do life on five hours of sleep.

One painfully accurate meme shows a cartoon rendering of the average human begging Jesus to "stop giving me your toughest battles," to which Jesus replies, "LOL. Just go to bed earlier." I detect no lies here, friends. But since I'm a big fan of God's *actual* words, let's look at Psalm 127:2, which says, "It is in vain that you rise up early and go late to rest, eating the bread of anxious toil."

Accepting the Gift of Rest

To be fair, it's a tad generous to call half the things I do past 10:30 p.m. "anxious toil." More like "distracted, mindless scrolling" or "unfocused sentence writing that must be edited heavily the next day." But that's kind of the point, right? We don't do our best work or use our best judgment when we're tired. (And yes, I realize that some of us are night owls, but chances are, even if you do fantastic work at 2:00 a.m., the rest of the world is not on the same schedule as you, and you will still suffer the self-inflicted consequence of too little sleep and too much energy from your toddler.)

Chances are, even if you do fantastic work at 2:00 a.m., the rest of the world is not on the same schedule as you, and you will still suffer the self-inflicted consequence of too little sleep and too much energy from your toddler.

Thankfully, the rest of Psalm 127:2 is reassuring: "For he gives to his beloved sleep." No matter how much we try to convince ourselves that we couldn't possibly go to sleep yet, God is there, patiently holding out the gift of rest, if we'll only be wise enough to receive it.

One summer, our family took a trip (it's not a "vacation" if there are little kids involved) to Alaska. We were in a car or a plane for fourteen straight hours with ten children, ages twenty months to sixteen years. And when we arrived in the Land of the Midnight Sun, bleary-eyed and exhausted, it took several

HE GIVES TO HIS BELOVED SLEEP.

PSALM 127:2

days for our bodies to recover from the effects of the brutal travel schedule and adjust to the three-hour time difference and never-ending sunlight.

On our third morning there, I woke up even more disoriented than I had the previous two days. My head pulsed with pain and the room refused to stay right side up. With Shaun and the older boys heading out on a chartered fishing trip, I was dreading solo-parenting the eight younger children. So I lay down on the couch, which Titus took as an invitation to whomp me in the face with a plush dinosaur. When Shaun suggested I crawl back into bed until he and the big boys left, a prideful sliver of my soul resisted. *No thanks; I'll be just fine right here. A real woman can make it without a nap.*

Does anybody else think I'm an obstinate doofus but also know exactly what I'm talking about?

Instead, I nodded miserably and headed back to bed. Through the kind suggestion of my husband, the Lord had literally offered me, His beloved, sleep. I would have made my life unnecessarily harder (and been acting the fool) by refusing to accept it. Thankfully, when I woke up an hour later, the room was no longer tilting, and the younger kids and I proceeded to have a fantastic day of zoo visits and ice cream with a minimum of toddler meltdowns.

When We Fall Short of Our Own Standards

Of course, not getting enough sleep is hardly the only form of self-sabotage at which we excel. Another common (and uncomfortable) answer from my "self-inflicted hard" survey: setting an example for our children that we *don't* want them to follow.

The pitfalls of "do what I say, not what I do" are myriad. And "more is caught than taught" is so much more than a trite phrase. For years, my daughters struggled to keep their room clean, in large part because they saw their mama doing the same. It wasn't until I made my bedroom a priority and stayed on top of reminders to them (which I could finally do without feeling guilty for my own pigsty) that their habits began to change. The same goes for cleaning out our car, using wise time management, and being true to our word. And how convicting to hear your seven-year-old shushing his younger brother with an impatient phrase you know he heard from you!

When we catch our children committing the "sins of the mother," it's easy to sidestep blame—or at least look to our peers for justification. One DM I received from a young mom made my heart ache with sadness and empathy for both her and her little boy. She described at length her annoyance at his more frustrating traits and admitted that she struggled to even look at him. "He whines all the time, and I don't even like him," she said. "I know he's probably getting a lot of these habits from my example, but I just don't know how to change my attitude toward him. Am I the only one who feels this way?"

Justification in Christ Alone

Friend, you and I both know she's not. I truly believe that every mama who reads this book will, at some point in her mothering career, feel a moment (or maybe many) of hostility toward at least one of her own children. I know I have. And if we're honest, we must acknowledge that sometimes the sinful fruit we resent the most in our kids springs up from the seed of our own bad example.

Sometimes the sinful fruit we resent the most in our kids springs up from the seed of our own bad example.

In that moment of self-reflection, we have two choices:

1. Take a worldly stance of defensiveness and bravado. A letterboard meme I stumbled upon summed up this attitude with defiant accuracy: "Don't let that perfect-seeming Instagram mom fool you. Her kids are nasty little &%$@ just like yours. Just keep doing you."

2. Repent and ask the Lord for the strength to set a better example for our children. And then (and this is the biggest pill to swallow) ask our children to forgive us as well.

I know, on one level, that the mom who sent me that message about her son wanted me to affirm her anger as normal and acceptable, to exonerate her from any blame, to give her a pass to be justifiably annoyed. And I know this because without the transforming work of the Holy Spirit in our lives, we will all cling to our sin. Jesus said that "everyone who practices sin is a slave to sin" (John 8:34). Thankfully, we don't have to "clean ourselves up" before approaching the throne of grace. Jesus took care of that on the cross, for "while we were still sinners, Christ died for us" (Romans 5:8).

I believe, on another level, this desperate young mother was hoping I would give her something tangible to raise her out of the slough of despond (where my *Pilgrim's Progress* peeps at?) that threatened to color each of her mothering memories a dull gray of drudgery.

Baby Steps of Progress

Guess what, friends?

She had already taken a very practical step toward climbing out of the mire when she asked for advice. Often, the best thing we can do once we have acknowledged the mess of our own making is to find someone we trust. And *then* "listen to advice and accept instruction, that you may gain wisdom in the future. Many are the plans in the mind of man, but it is the purpose of the LORD that will stand" (Proverbs 19:20-21).

So what did I tell her to do? I encouraged her to go with option 2 from above: repentance and acceptance of the grace and biblical wisdom God offers so freely. I encourage every mama I encounter to do the same, not because I am perfectly consistent in forsaking sin or because I never make wrong choices, but because I have been the happy recipient of the kindness of the Lord that leads to repentance (Romans 2:4) too many times to *not* want others to experience the same.

Join the Club

Do you doubt yourself as a mother? Your ability to choose rightly? To stay the course? To set a righteous example for the kiddos you love more than life itself? To avoid shooting yourself in the foot?

Well, join the club of Christian Sisters Who Make Our Lives Hard with Poor Life Choices but Also Know God's Grace Is Sufficient for Our Sin (that would make one doozy of an acronym, I realize—I'll work on it). Remember, we are new creations in Christ (2 Corinthians 5:17), which means His power at work in us enables us to walk forward into better disciplines and godlier habits as we recognize and reject our old, fleshly routines.

Yes, hard is not the same thing as bad. But that's no excuse to carry on with a stressful habit that is harming us, our families, and the peace of our homes. In fact, the best part about self-imposed hardship is the way it forces us to partake of the goodness of the gospel on a daily basis.

After all, "Shall we go on sinning so that grace may increase? *By no means!*" (Romans 6:1-2 NIV, emphasis added).

But shall we go on repenting and growing when we do get it wrong? *Absolutely!*

PUTTING IT INTO PRACTICE

I know some of you are just itching to fire off an email asking me for specific ways to avoid heaping trouble on our own heads, so I thought I'd include a short list here of wisdom I've gleaned from others and insights the Lord has revealed to me over the last almost eighteen years of motherhood—simple (but not always easy) ways to avoid wandering into the thorniest trenches of motherhood.

- *Bible-reading.* I know. So basic. Except, are you doing it consistently and with an attitude of learning rather than checking a box? If you need more structure, I suggest the inductive Bible study method, the *NLT One Year Chronological Bible Creative Expressions* (after being an ESV or NASB girl most of my life, I have been surprised by how much I've loved this translation with the journaling component), or *The Bible Recap* (in either print or podcast form, or both).

- *Accountability.* Don't feel like you can get to bed earlier, memorize Scripture, or kick an anger habit on your own? You'd be amazed at the motivation and encouragement afforded by a good friend who's willing to pray for and hold you accountable to do the things you say you will.

- *Handwritten lists.* Sure, it's low-tech, but there's something incredibly propelling (and satisfying) about physically crossing through an item on a to-do list—even if you write the task after it's already done! Plus, it's always better to write things down than to have a jumble of "probably shoulds" rattling around in your brain.

- *Timers, alarms, reminders.* We live in an era of constantly evolving technology. We can literally yell from across the room, "Alexa, remind me to water the plants at 3:00 p.m." and she will. We can set a fifteen-minute cleaning timer and race to see how much we can get done before it goes off (you'll probably shock yourself by how much you accomplish).

- *Cleaning schedules.* I'm always a little surprised by questions like "How do you know what day you should vacuum your rugs?" Besides the obvious answer of "When they're dirty," the easiest way to get to a task is to put it on a regular rotation for a particular day of the week. If Monday is "bathroom day," then you know you'll get a clean toilet at least once a week. (If you don't know when you should clean what, resources like flylady.net or cleanmama.com have *free* tools to help get you organized.)

- *Decent bedtimes!* I know we already mentioned this, but sleep really is our friend.

- *Wisdom—starting with God, then your husband, then a trusted counselor.* Too often, I see this order completely reversed. Someone will ask *me* for advice in a direct message before she's prayed about it, talked to her own husband, or sought out godly counsel from a face-to-face source.

⌒ DAD THOUGHT ⌒

At the end of chapter 5, I discussed the father's role as the family cruise control, the need to avoid coasting as a result of our protective braking, and the calling to "run the race" and grow in our capacity to handle hard things.

Fortunately, as a counterpart to our protective natures, we also tend to have high ambition and tolerance for risk-taking that can serve as an accelerator that pushes us and our families to excel. Of course, just as we can over-protect, we can easily find ourselves in single-minded pursuit of a goal and miss the weary strain in our wife's voice or the wild-eyed look in the eyes of our over-stimulated or under-attended children.

While Abbie and I were on an anniversary trip, strolling leisurely down a boardwalk on a beautiful evening, a man passed us on a bicycle and brayed, "PUMP YOUR BRAKES, SASSAFRAS!" After a few startled moments of "Sassafras? Who's Sassafras, and why do they need to pump their brakes? Wait, are *we* Sassafras?" we realized he was hollering at a female companion we hadn't noticed. For the rest of the day, we took turns randomly shouting, "Pump your brakes, Sassafras!" and then dissolving into laughter. To this day, we use this ridiculous phrase anytime we notice one of us getting ahead of ourselves or trying to do too much.

It's just the reminder we need when we're being "gluttons for punishment" by taking on all the things at once.

Just as driving too fast can keep us from recognizing dangers in time to avoid a collision, saying yes to more than we have time for can wreck our family's peace.

Margin is crucial—enough margin to be able to reflect on God's Word and will and to recognize the warning signs of a family fraying at the edges. Without this margin, we risk losing control, overcorrecting, and straying off His path.

Let's remember that "whoever makes haste with his feet misses his way" (Proverbs 19:2) and, when we realize we're carelessly charging ahead, remind ourselves to "pump the brakes, Sassafras" so that we may stay on the straight and narrow.

 **The Narrative**

THE WORLD'S RESPONSE TO HARD	A CHRISTIAN RESPONSE TO HARD
Can always find someone else to blame for struggles	Takes responsibility for unwise decisions
Clings to the very sin that is creating chaos	Repents of the bad choices that steal peace from our homes
Seeks validation rather than godly counsel	Is open to good advice about how to keep from causing unnecessary hardship in our homes

 **Action Steps**

- Memorize and meditate on Proverbs 19:20-21: "Listen to advice and accept instruction, that you may gain wisdom in the future. Many are the plans in the mind of man, but it is the purpose of the LORD that will stand."

- Identify two ways in which you might be the architect of your own misery (hard situations, suffering, discomfort).

- Write down three things (setting timers, going to bed earlier, memorizing verses) that could help you begin to break away from those unhelpful habits. Let your accountability partner know about your plans.

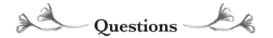

Questions

Why do we sometimes continue in unwise practices even though they cause us so many problems?

What does the Bible have to say about wise decision-making? (You can do internet searches like "verses about wisdom," "time management," or "good choices" for a quick dive into this topic.)

Who benefits the most when we shift to a mindset of overcomer in Christ from one of victimhood to our own bad choices?

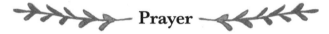

Prayer

Jesus, You are perfect and sinless, and yet You chose to "seek not my own will but the will of him who sent me" (John 5:30). Convict our hearts to emulate Your example instead of clinging to bad habits (simply because they are comfortable) that are harming the peace of our homes.

> If you need a reset in your ability to use kind speech and calm tones, consider a thirty-day commitment to the Gentleness Challenge. I detail this at length in *M Is for Mama*, and in my step-by-step ebook, available at misformama.net/downloads/the-gentleness-challenge.

7

When We Can't Escape the Hard

LOOKING FOR GOD'S GOODNESS WHEN WE FEEL STUCK

What were you thinking, getting pregnant with twins?" I stared, mouth ajar at such a bizarre question, as this "church lady" on a Sunday morning fixed my protruding belly with a stare and waited for me to explain myself. I was six months pregnant with Evy and Nola, our numbers four and five, feeling nervous and excited to meet them. But now I also felt confused, not simply because the question made no sense (um, ma'am, you might want to take up the issue of spontaneous twins with God, not me) but because this woman also had five children, including not one, but *two sets* of spontaneous twins.

Like, what?

God's Wisdom > Man's Wisdom

The thing is, this wasn't just a hard I had done nothing to "deserve." It was, in fact, a hard I had prayed fervently against—the kind of "Dear God, please give me the children You have for me, except not multiples because those sound really difficult, 'kay, thanks, amen" petition that *might* not be included in any volume of *Most Selfless and Faith-Filled Prayers of the Saints.*

Did God listen? No, He did not.

Not only did He give me one set of identical twins, but then, eight years later, He gave me another set.

And I'm so glad! Both my identical twin girls, Evangeline and Magnolia, and my identical twin boys, Titus and Tobias, represent some of the most potent forces for sanctification, joy, and God's goodness in my life.

They're also a perfect exemplification of a verse I love so much that I put it to song way back in my teen Christian grunge band days. It goes like this:

> Oh, the depth of the riches and wisdom and knowledge of God! How unsearchable are his judgments and how inscrutable his ways! "For who has known the mind of the Lord, or who has been his counselor?" "Or who has given a gift to him that he might be repaid?" For from him and through him and to him are all things. To him be glory forever. Amen (Romans 11:33-36).

Just *how* unsearchable are God's judgments?

Friends, let me tell you.

As you can imagine, we get asked a fair bit if twins run in our family, but the fact is identical mono/di twins (one placenta, two amniotic sacs) are not hereditary. They occur by pure "chance" (otherwise known as divine design) when one fertilized egg splits into two. Try as they might, the medical community has been unable to establish a consensus for why one woman would be more likely than another to get pregnant with twins in this serendipitous fashion, and yet I have been pregnant with mono/di multiples not once, not twice, but *three* times (although we lost Theo's brother to vanishing twin syndrome at eight weeks).

If you're looking for a number to go with the unlikelihood of such a statistical anomaly, the odds are 1 in 27 million.

That's how inscrutable God's ways are.

So in answer to the church lady's question, what I was thinking when I got pregnant with twins was something like "Well, Lord, You must know what You're doing because I sure don't. But I trust You anyway."

Better, Not Easier

Here's the thing: I've just declared what an incredibly good gift both of my sets of twins are, and that is true. But I've also acknowledged that this in no way means they've made our lives *easier*. (Remember Evy and Nola's propensity for turning our car rides into the equivalent of a toddler thrash metal session?)

A reader once asked me how infant twins compare to having two small children under two years old. I had to chuckle, because both times I had twin babies, I *also* had a small child under the age of two. So my view is skewed. Perhaps I should instead answer in the words of another reader: "I have two that are sixteen months apart. My sister has twins. One day, I kept her twins, thinking I'd rock it after being a mom to two so close together. And let me tell you, twins kicked my tail!"

As a mother whose first two were eighteen months and three days apart, I know exactly what she means. Two babies with the exact same needs and developmental limitations (neither can talk! walk! go potty! feed himself!) is a completely different challenge than one newborn and a child who can fetch a diaper or hold his own sippy cup. And while I'm happy to report that not every stage has felt twice as hard as it did for their singleton siblings, some did.

In fact, some twin stages felt about five times harder than with singletons. Like those weeks of nights when Shaun and I lay limply in bed, holding a paci apiece in Titus's and Toby's mouths, trying to sleep deeply enough to be unconscious but not deeply enough to release the pacifier, only to drop like stones into such bottomless slumber that we jerked awake to the sound of wailing, unplugged babies. All. Night. Long.

We All Need Jesus for Our Hard

And I say that knowing that two sleepless newborns hold up not even the dimmest candle to the health and behavioral parenting challenges that some of you dear readers have endured. But "hardship checks" (you know, where you hold your struggle bus cards up to your neighbor's and compare the score) rarely produce more than a flare of pride or despair before we must acknowledge that, equal or not, we all need Jesus for our hard. And let me tell you, navigating life with eight children plus two newborns on nothing but the tattered rags of three hours of sleep had me singing and living "I Need Thee Every Hour."

The thing that left the deepest impression from both Evy and Nola's angsty toddler phase and Titus and Toby's sleep-striking first year was the constant nature of the energy drain. There was no "pass the baby off to Daddy for an hour" (although Shaun pitched in heartily whenever possible, especially with our second set of twins). Because, even in those moments when rest might have been possible, there were always two—one for him, one for me. (Whenever Shaun and I see people with triplets or quads, we just shake our heads in awe. That is the big league.) While the twinbies' older siblings are incredibly helpful and precious with babies, they're also just kids, and we never want them to feel like they, rather than we, are ultimately responsible for this good but hard blessing the Lord has given their parents.

In other words, the gift of multiples feels a bit, well, relentless at times. It's why, as horrifying as I find the practice, it's not uncommon for an ob-gyn to ask women expecting multiples, even those experiencing completely healthy pregnancies, if they'd like to practice "selective reduction" (a.k.a. end the life of one or more of the babies). Thankfully, I have never been offered such an option (both because my care providers were Christian midwives and because it's much less likely to be offered for mono/di twins). The bald-faced nature of the suggestion that, since one baby is logistically easier than two, a woman might be better off murdering one of her own children to keep her hard more "manageable" shines a lurid spotlight on the deeply held postmodern cultural view that we should flee from the hard, whenever possible—and that our lives (and our children's lives) are our own to do with as we please.

Remaining Steadfast

I hope we, as Christian mothers, can all agree that infanticide is not the answer when the going gets tough and we doubt our capacity to mother well.

So, as Bible-believing followers of Christ, what *should* we do when our circumstances or convictions mean that hardship is *inescapable*?

We have to look no further for our answer than James 1:12, which says, "Blessed is the man who remains steadfast under trial, for when he has stood the test he will receive the crown of life, which God has promised to those who love him."

All right, then. Thanks, James. You made that simple.

But wait a minute. That verse says nothing about this life, except for the "steadfast under trials" part. And that doesn't sound too fun. What do we get *in this earthly realm* that makes all this suffering worthwhile or even possible to withstand?

Well, in the case of both my sets of twins, the answer is obvious: I get double the slobbery, open-mouthed kisses, twice the chubby-armed hugs, two times the cheerful, girlish chatter, twice the cheeks flecked with gorgeous constellations of ginger freckles. Some twin stages feel relentless, yes, but others feel like the best kind of surprise bonus (I can't tell you how many times Shaun and I have grinned at each other and said, "Isn't it the coolest that there are two of them!").

It's not too difficult (some days) to see the "payback" for the hard in our children because the Lord is so gracious to fill our mother hearts with an aching love that threatens to burst us at the seams and flood the world with how much we adore our babies. (Again, *some days*.)

The Lord is so gracious to fill our mother hearts with an aching love that threatens to burst us at the seams and flood the world with how much we adore our babies.

Blessed is the man who remains steadfast under trial, for when he has stood the test he will receive the crown of life, which God has promised to those who love him.

JAMES 1:12

A Crucible of Love

But there are other hards that are just as tenacious, just as unavoidable, and with these we must dig even deeper to find the treasure. As Proverbs 17:3 reminds us, "The crucible is for silver, and the furnace is for gold, and the LORD tests hearts."

One such heart-testing reality is the fact that my dad is bipolar.

I have never written these words, although I have said them to trusted friends. I'm hesitant to "speak" them now, knowing that some who read will be neither friendly nor trustworthy. But I feel compelled to share about a dad who grapples with mental illness because his struggles are the kind of inescapable hard that has, at times, felt like the opposite of good. And yet the Lord has been faithful through this crucible to reveal the dross of my own hardheartedness and the silver and gold of glimpses into my heavenly Father's affection for me through my dad's efforts to connect.

My earthly father loves me. I know this now, even though I was convinced of the contrary for much of my life. But he came with little in his toolbox to make him capable of expressing his love in most conventional ways.

During my early childhood, we mostly connected through sports. Sometimes this connection was clear and strong. Other times, it was full of static. My dad would devote hours to hitting fly balls for me to snag in the outfield. He taught me to "throw like a boy" (high praise in his book). He still proudly tells the story of the time I, at six years old, made an unassisted triple play in T-ball, simply because he'd drilled me so thoroughly in the rules and skills of the game that I was able to catch a pop-up, then tag two runners out at their bases before any of the other understandably clueless first graders registered their coaches' frantic cries of "TAG UP!" We watched game after game of hockey and football together. His teams were my teams, his favorite players mine, even when I couldn't begin to tell you what a tight end or a cornerback actually did.

Of course, he would also throw the ball whether or not I was looking and, if it thwacked hard into my temple, he'd tell me I should pay better attention next time. Even before his diagnosis, empathy was never his strong suit.

Flawed but Trying

He worked long hours as a derrick man in the oil field—a menial, thankless job for which he often drove over an hour one way to a twelve-hour shift. And yet on his infrequent days off, he always came to my competitions when he could—soccer, softball, basketball, volleyball, and swimming.

Mostly though, I remember what my dad's hard work and intentional sacrifice gave me and my brother: my mom's presence. Even though she had her master's degree in English and my dad dropped out before graduating from college, both my parents had pledged they would do everything they could to allow her to stay home and teach my older brother and me. Far from subscribing to the second-wave feminist ideologies touted by my mom's four aunts, who told her she was "wasting" her degree by staying home with us, my parents felt convicted to swim upstream against the way the culture thought we should be "socialized." Having both become Christians in either their teens or young adulthood, they felt a pull to abandon the neglectful, abusive practices of their upbringings.

A quick look at some of my paternal grandparents' less admirable traits helps explain why my dad lacked gentleness and compassion. His parents were weighed down by baggage of their own. My philandering grandfather would leave pornographic magazines in full view, heedless of the warping effects on his five young boys' minds. My grandmother—herself a de facto orphan—struggled with alcoholism. My mom came from a similarly fraught home environment with a father who regularly reminded her, in the most profane terms possible, what a burden she was and a mother who often struggled to get out of bed to face the day (largely in response to her husband's harshness).

Smashing the Links

My parents' backgrounds underscore just how abrupt an about-face God called them to make in raising my brother and me with intention and focused effort. Notice I did not say perfection. None of us will get that from anyone but our heavenly Father. But He used my mother and father as sledgehammers to smash crucial links in the chains of generational bondage that held their forefathers. My parents fought early and hard to ensure my brother and I would have a different story to tell our children, who will, in turn, be able to tell their own children a different story still.

Being homeschooled by my mother and being read the Bible on a regular basis by my father are the two early foundational constants that molded my most basic and formative views of family and God. I will never stop thanking Jesus that my dad valued keeping my mom home with her young children enough that he persevered in a grueling career, despite meager salaries and the kind of strain on his body that precipitated two knee replacements by the age of sixty. Because of my mom's steady, loving presence and my father's dogged work, I never felt deprived of the most needful things.

My father's commitment to turning the tide for his own family produced tangible results in my life and will have a trickle-down effect for many generations to come. I am intentional to acknowledge his efforts because if I'm not, I can fall victim to the oh-so-human tendency to sweep up the scraps (or even whole banquets) of goodness with the jagged shards of frustration and hurt and throw them all in the same wastebasket of broken relationships.

Beyond that, I share to bring encouragement to those of *you* whom God has tasked with beginning to dismantle links of addiction or neglect or abuse or godlessness in your own family chain. This incredibly hard calling of being the first to hack your way through the briars of bad habits and generational curses is *crucial* because your children, by God's grace, will get to experience more freedom from the lingering effects of their ancestors' sins.

Looking for the Goodness of God

During periods in my life when I have been the most despondent about my dad's inability to just "be normal," the Lord has continually reminded me of Psalm 27:13 (NIV), which says, "I remain confident of this: I will see the goodness of the LORD in the land of the living." Even when circumstances spiraled beyond my control, and hope for change felt like a bit of flotsam just beyond my drowning reach, I could choose to remember that the very same father who pierced my heart with barbed words and angered me with his careless actions in his manic states was the one who had occasionally taken my brother and me on "field-trip sleepovers" to the oil rig during his night shifts when we were young and gave me the last bit of hot mint tea from his thermos before I drifted off to sleep on a makeshift pallet in the trailer office.

I can look back now and recognize moments in my childhood when my frustration with my dad's actions resulted from his being in a manic state (even though, at the time, I simply found him "annoying" and responded by shrugging off or sneering at his behavior). But it wasn't until my teens, when my dad's mental and physical health began to deteriorate and my mom went to work full-time to keep our family financially afloat, that I began to feel trapped by his erratic behavior.

I became engaged to my first and only (up to that point) boyfriend at nineteen. I still remember the day he told me he'd been offered a position in Idaho Falls. I was the opposite of thrilled. But my first panicked thought had nothing to do with the harsh winters or the relational isolation of not knowing a soul. No. My immediate worry was: "How could I move 1,500 miles away and leave my mom alone with my dad's struggles?"

The engagement ultimately faltered under the strain of this worry, among other factors, and I found myself hoping and praying, yet again, for the "goodness of the Lord in the land of the living." (Little did I know what an incredibly good husband He was preparing for me as I waited.)

During my senior year in college, as I navigated the stress of planning a wedding, graduating at nineteen from college (thanks to homeschooling), landing a teaching job I'd probably have to abandon halfway through the year if I moved to Idaho, and trying to provide support to my family in an increasingly unstable home environment, I was more overloaded than overcoming.

Although I'm pretty sure I failed miserably at almost all of the relational aspects from that list above, by God's grace, I still graduated summa cum laude and transitioned into a job teaching high school Spanish to students who were only a year younger than I was. I dropped fifteen pounds without trying in those months leading up to the wedding that never happened, and although I only vaguely remember this, my mom tells me she would regularly find me curled in the fetal position on my bed, staring blankly at the wall. To say this is unlike me is like saying it's unusual to find a pregnant woman who doesn't crave sweets.

I'm typically a doer, not a worrier. But I worried plenty that year.

More Is Too Much

My dad's manic episodes continued to ramp up steadily (not uncommon with age), resulting in more familial stress and more personal hurt. Some of those old wounds still throb at times. Some are scabs systematically picked open by his continued manic episodes (especially for my mother and brother). For me, most have scarred over with time and prayer and maturity. One of the ways God has revealed His goodness to me "in the land of the living" is in the softening of my heart. He's given me empathy for others who struggle with similarly complicated relationships, the kind that feel like stepping into a bear trap and realizing that in addition to the mangled mess you've made of your foot, you might also break an ankle getting it back out again.

But empathy is not the same thing as indulging in all the unnecessary details. Anytime I have even hinted at a less-than-ideal father figure, my inbox gets flooded with requests for information, for validation, for confirmation of damage, for similarity of experience.

For *more*.

But I truly believe that more is not really mine to give.

Chances are, in an ancient culture in which privacy was at a minimum, Noah's sons, Shem and Japheth, knew exactly what their father looked like naked. And yet when Noah gets drunk and takes off all his clothes in his tent, they "took a garment and laid it across their shoulders; then they walked in backward and covered their father's naked body" (Genesis 9:23 NIV).

Their refusal to "expose" him further in his inebriated (shameful) state shows an admirable understanding of a law of the Lord that didn't get literally written in stone for many years to come: "'Honor your father and mother' (which is the first commandment with a promise), 'that it may go well with you and that you may have a long life on the earth'" (Ephesians 6:2-3 BSB, quoting Deuteronomy 5:16). And I say this after having submitted both this chapter and the following one to my parents for approval and edits and then engaging in weeks of agonizing, prayerful rewrites to make sure I "got this right." (They both gave their blessing to publish it.)

Protecting, Not Pretending

Clearly, if it were "dishonorable" to acknowledge that people are sinful, we would never even know that Noah made a fool of himself in front of his family. The Bible would not be full of cautionary parenting tales like Eli, Samuel, David, Solomon, and three-quarters of Israel's and Judah's other kings. Pretending that flawed parents (or husbands or children or wives) are perfect can be just as harmful as airing every detail of dirty laundry to the public in a desperate bid for commiseration. But the guiding principle of Scripture is that we refuse to unnecessarily expose our parents' (or anyone else's) shortcomings in favor of practicing the admonition in 1 Peter 4:8 (BSB) to "love one another deeply, because love covers over a multitude of sins."

Pretending that flawed parents (or husbands or children or wives) are perfect can be just as harmful as airing every detail of dirty laundry to the public in a desperate bid for commiseration.

There have been times that, far from desiring to cover my father's sins with love, I have felt nothing but hatred for him. Yet today, despite his continued battle with bipolarism, I believe, more than ever, in the goodness of the Lord in the land of the living, and I believe that His sovereign working and timing are worth waiting for (the word "wait" in Hebrew is the same as the one for hope). For "hope does not put us to shame, because God's love has been poured into our hearts through the Holy Spirit who has been given to us" (Romans 5:5).

Thankfully, "when you write from a healed scar rather than an open wound, you offer your readers hope." I'll talk more about this hope in the next chapter, but here's a hint: Often, when we find ourselves stuck in a struggle from which we can find no escape, forgiveness is the only key that has the power to unlock the prison of bitterness and set us free.

Often, when we find ourselves stuck in a struggle from which we can find no escape, forgiveness is the only key that has the power to unlock the prison of bitterness and set us free.

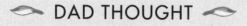

My mom is bipolar.

Like Abbie, I have never typed those words before. And though I don't have the space here to expound on the details of how this fact shaped my childhood, I write it now to point out an important truth about those inescapable hards: They are often used for a good that is impossible to see in the midst of the struggle—a good we may not realize until much later in life (if ever).

Could I have known, while confronting the reality of my own mother's contemplating suicide, that my future bride's father would be bipolar?

No.

Did either of us truly grasp what we were learning about coping with bipolarism? Or confronting the ugliness of our own sinful responses to these extremes of human emotion?

Nope.

Did we grasp the work the Lord was doing in us by teaching us to separate the effects of our parents' illness from their genuine love for us?

Still no.

Did we fully appreciate the examples of continued love, perseverance, and dependability that our respective non-bipolar parents set for us?

Not completely, no.

Despite these examples (both good and bad), do we still perpetuate some of our parents' failings and add others of our own?

Yes.

And yet we have the privilege of looking back to see what God knew all along: Our common experiences in childhood would grant understanding and shared perspective to our future marriage. They would allow us to continue the work of breaking generational curses that our parents began. We share our experience with you "so that we may be able to comfort those who are in any affliction, with the comfort with which we ourselves are comforted by God" (2 Corinthians 1:4).

It may not make an inescapable hard any easier or more palatable at the time, but knowing that "for those who love God all things work together for good, for those who are called according to his purpose" (Romans 8:28), can surely bring hope and comfort.

 **The Narrative**

THE WORLD'S RESPONSE TO HARD	A CHRISTIAN RESPONSE TO HARD
Looks for a way out of all hard relationships	Stays invested in God-ordained relationships despite the cost
Views pain as random and meaningless	Believes that in Christ, all things work together for good for the believer
Sees only the negative in a "stuck" situation	Looks for growth within the hardship

 **Action Steps**

- Memorize and meditate on Psalm 27:13 (NIV): "I remain confident of this: I will see the goodness of the LORD in the land of the living."

- If a particular "inescapable hard" came to mind as you read this chapter, take some time to ask the Lord to show you ways this situation has been a force for good in your life (even if it's just in demonstrating your need for Jesus).

- Ask the Lord to remind you of someone who might need encouragement that their inescapable hard is not hopeless and that they will still see the goodness of the Lord in the land of the living. Then send them a text or a note or a meal—anything to let them know God has not forgotten them.

Questions

Why do you think the word for "wait" is the same as the word for "hope" in the Hebrew language?

What are some of the good things the Lord revealed to you about your seasons of "inescapable hardship"?

Why is honoring parents and covering over sin with love such a theme in the Bible?

Prayer

Lord, we acknowledge that every good and perfect gift comes from You (James 1:17). Help us to shift our mindset from one of resentment to one of looking for the good as we encounter hardship from which we cannot escape in this lifetime. When we struggle to find joy in the present, help us to be mindful of the joy that is coming in the future.

8

The Hard Work of Forgiveness

IT HAS THE POWER TO CHANGE THE WAY WE MOTHER

I watch my three-year-old shriek gleefully, giggles bubbling out of him like the fizz from a shaken soda bottle, his rosebud lips stretched wide, his baby teeth gleaming. And I can't help but smile with him. How could I not when Shiloh's joy pulses in almost tangible waves from the trampoline where he plays "tickle spider" with Sabba (my children's "grandpa name" for my dad)? It radiates across the yard and through the kitchen window where I stand, rinsing dishes at the sink, tears dripping from my nose into the soapy water.

This moment feels like a gift. A tiny bit of restoration for all the years the locusts of dysfunction have eaten (Joel 2:25). And it feels this way because I can enjoy it without hostility, without a "yeah, but" or a "he never."

Instead, I can simply bask in the knowledge that my toddler's memories of Sabba need never be tainted with a caveat of disappointment.

A Gradual Freedom

For years I was plagued by constant bitterness toward my dad. Freedom from that attitude came not in a "road to Damascus" moment of blinding clarity. Not in an altar call or a counseling appointment. Not even in one of many late-night, hash-it-out, what-to-do sessions with my mom and brother. Instead, it was more like a dawning. The light starts low and weak on the horizon, then gradually grows bolder, creeping forward, strengthening every moment, until finally we find ourselves noting with surprise, "It's morning!"

I have no doubt that the Lord used time and less contact with my dad to effect much of the change He wrought in me.

It's different for everyone. The first time I told my mom I had forgiven my dad, she said, "I'm not sure forgiveness is an event. I think it's more like something you have to keep choosing until the day you die." My brother, who lives next door to my parents, has echoed her thoughts. I don't disagree. And I know that I would feel this way so much more acutely if I still lived with or very near my dad and bore the brunt of his struggles like they do. I have no doubt that the Lord used time and less contact with my dad to effect much of the change He wrought in me.

I can still feel hurt and intense anger, and while I have to ask the Lord to "create in me a new heart" each time I feel my hackles rising again, I can also say that for me and for this situation, I no longer harbor an ever-present, festering, gangrenous wound of resentment. And the moment I realized this shift had taken place? It felt like unwrapping a surprise birthday present to find something you've had your eye on for so long but never dreamed you'd actually receive.

I don't remember the exact day, but I do recall a sensation of lightness, of almost giddiness, that after praying for release from resentment for so many years, it arrived. Not in an epic wrestling with God that left me limping but in a gentle whisper of "You're free." The limp is there just the same. It never quite goes away due to the cyclical nature of my dad's condition. But thanks to time, distance, and the Lord's gracious answer to my prayers, it no longer cripples me. And I can claim no credit for that.

It Was My Sin for Which Jesus Died

If you just went back to reread the title of this chapter and thought, "The hard work of forgiveness? What you're describing doesn't sound too hard, Abbie. I think you might have taken the 'forgiveness lite' course," let me just say that one glance at my journal entries about my dad from my twenties would disabuse you of this notion completely. I *battled* to reconcile what I knew to be true from Scripture with the way my emotions raged and gnashed their teeth at me every time I so much as thought of him.

After all, I'd been a Christian since age five when I excitedly pledged my heart to Jesus while listening to *Bullfrogs and Butterflies* with my best friend in her playroom one sweltering summer afternoon. I know the "sinner's prayer" is out of vogue, but my desire to repent was genuine, if childlike. I understood, in the most basic way a child can, that it was my sin for which Jesus died.

As the Lord grew me up in Him, I gleaned more knowledge about the ugly nature of my sin and why Jesus's sacrifice for it was so necessary: "He himself bore our sins in his body on the tree, that we might die to sin and live to righteousness. By his wounds you have been healed" (1 Peter 2:24).

Also, "*All* have sinned and fall short of the glory of God, and are justified by his grace as a gift, through the redemption that is in Christ Jesus" (Romans 3:23-24, emphasis added).

And again, "If you forgive others their trespasses, your heavenly Father will also forgive you, but if you do not forgive others their trespasses, neither will your Father forgive your trespasses" (Matthew 6:14-15).

I could keep going with at least fifty more verses about the heaviness of our own sin and the responsibility we have to forgive others as God in Christ forgave us (Ephesians 4:32). The very man whom I struggled (and often failed) to honor was the one who taught many of those verses to me.

The Unbalanced Scale of God's Forgiveness

I knew it was my own unyielding heart of unforgiveness that lay at the root of my angst. After all, no amount of provocation from my father could create anything new in me. It could only reveal the depths of mockery and self-righteousness that lurked in the darkest corners of my heart. And yet. Despite my head knowledge of the right thing to do (and often a genuine desire to do it!), my unruly feelings bucked and bristled at the implication that my dad—himself a Christian—deserved exactly the same degree of forgiveness the Lord had so freely offered me.

On the one hand, this is natural. It makes perfect *human* sense to see the discrepancy between behavior and belief and think, "Wow, Lord. I would *not* let them get away with that." In our flesh, we are convinced that, if it were our job to balance the scales, we'd have those bad boys dead even.

It's hardly a "modern" problem, either.

Way back in Matthew 20, we see our universal tendency to self-justify in Jesus's parable of the laborers in the vineyard. A landowner needs help, so he goes out early in the day, finds men loafing around, offers them a fair wage, and puts them to work in his vineyard. As the day progresses, the master adds more workers to the job for the same pay until, just before quitting time, a few men squeak in the door to labor for only one hour.

Naturally (my fairness-loving soul can so relate to this, friends), as they watched the men who worked one measly hour receive the same pay they were offered for a full day, the men who labored longest began to hope for more money. When, instead, the master offered them the same "lousy" salary they had already agreed to, rumbles of mutiny erupted. "These last worked only one hour, and you have made them equal to us who have borne the burden of the day and the scorching heat" (Matthew 20:12).

That's not fair.

I have always been a "good girl." I don't smoke. I don't do drugs. I don't drink. I don't curse. I don't watch pornography. My husband is the only sexual partner I have ever had. I'm pretty squeaky clean on paper. Compare this with my father's tumultuous teen years filled with substance abuse, and one might be tempted to tip the scales in my favor because, surely, Christ used more of His atoning blood on the cross for my father's sins than for mine.

None Is Righteous

Except it doesn't work that way at all. The Bible makes it very clear that Christ died not only for our drunkenness, our adultery, and our violence but also for our laziness, our "bitter jealousy and selfish ambition," and our pride (James 3:14). Or in the words of Romans 3:11-12, "None is righteous, no, not one; no one understands; no one seeks for God. All have turned aside; together they have become worthless; no one does good, not even one."

Christ died not only for our drunkenness, our adultery, and our violence but also for our laziness, our "bitter jealousy and selfish ambition," and our pride.

Well, gee, Paul. Do you think you said "no one" and "not one" enough times? We all need Jesus. We get it.

But do we?

Or are we content, like the rich young ruler, to quietly coddle our favorite sins in private? "My covetousness only put a stripe on Jesus's back; it didn't kill him." Isn't that a version of what we tell ourselves? As noted in Mark 10:22, this wealthy young man "went away sorrowful" when Jesus challenged him to sell all he owned and give it to the poor. This upstanding member of the Jewish community was convinced he would ace the test of piety because he, like many of us, looked "so good" on paper. And when he failed, as every one of us will, he discovered he didn't truly love goodness nearly so much as the appearance of it.

Jesus doesn't care about "life résumés." He cares about "a broken and contrite heart."

Turns out, Jesus doesn't care about "life résumés." He cares about "a broken and contrite heart" (Psalm 51:17).

And for years I was the daughter with the heart full of a love and desire for God that warred with an irritation that He would, in His great mercy and forbearance, wash my earthly father just as clean as the daughter, when the daughter had surely taken so much less scrubbing.

Oh, friends. The presumption of thinking that some of us, with our avoidance of "obvious" sins (while the stubborn, hateful ones lie nestled in our hearts), deserve anything other than death and punishment is not lost on God. In fact, the parable of the laborers concludes with the master asking the disgruntled workers this exquisitely uncomfortable question: "Am I not allowed to do what I choose with what belongs to me? Or do you begrudge my generosity?" (Matthew 20:15).

The Hypocrisy of Unforgiveness

Paul keeps right on poking at the tender underbelly of our hypocrisy when he challenges fellow Christians with this scathing query: "Do you suppose... you who judge those who practice such things and yet do them yourself—that you will escape the judgment of God?" (Romans 2:3).

Ouch.

And C.S. Lewis just keeps the conviction coming: "To be a Christian means to forgive the inexcusable because God has forgiven the inexcusable in you."

If you're thinking, "Easier said than done, dude," well, me too. Maybe it'll comfort you as much as it does me to know that Paul grappled with mastery of sin too. I have found, just like Paul, that "although I want to do good, evil is right there with me. For in my inner being I delight in God's law; but I see another law at work in me, waging war against the law of my mind and making me a prisoner of the law of sin at work within me. What a wretched man I am! Who will rescue me from this body that is subject to death? Thanks be to God, who delivers me through Jesus Christ our Lord!" (Romans 7:21-25 NIV).

My emancipation from bitterness took place after years of the Lord being gracious (yes, *gracious*) enough to reveal how easy I was on my own sin and to peel away layers of subconscious reliance on my own "goodness." (If you had asked me if I actively thought I was good, I would for sure have said, "NO!" and meant it.) Much later, my emotions were finally ready to catch up with the truth I preached to myself and my children on the daily: "For by grace you have been saved through faith. And this is not your own doing; it is the gift of God, not a result of works, so that no one may boast" (Ephesians 2:8-9).

> *Our heavenly Father has enough grace to go around for every type of sin and every type of sinner who repents.*

We can't outearn our neighbor in the grace department. On the flip side, neither can we spend less of God's grace than someone else, then save up the excess for the weeks we haven't brought our A game. Our heavenly Father has enough grace to go around for every type of sin and every type of sinner who repents. And so, on those days when we feel like She-Ra, Princess of Power, we must commit to clinging just as tightly to the parachute of His grace as we do on the days when we feel like one of Cinderella's wicked stepsisters.

Seventy-Seven Times

So much of my ongoing journey toward consistently *feeling* like I have forgiven my father, once and for all, stems from the cyclical nature of bipolarism and my own lack of emotional self-regulation. My brother has likened it to having a nasty cut that, just when it begins to heal, has the Band-Aid ripped from its tender flesh. Again and again. It's easy to be nice to people who treat us well. When my dad is calm, it *feels* like I've forgiven him because I no longer struggle to return his goodwill (this was not always true in the years I remained angry with him even when he was even-keeled). But when he tips over into mania, my blood pressure mounts and my "triggered" brain sputters, "Here we go again!" When my emotions boil, I must acknowledge my reactionary tendencies and beg the Lord to "keep watch over the door of my lips" (Psalm 141:3), or something ungodly *will* march right out. There's nothing emotionally "one and done" about repeated patterns of hurtful actions that always seem to surface in the most stressful seasons. We need a supernatural watchguard, which we have in the Holy Spirit.

The Bible doesn't let us off the hook of the need to offer forgiveness *again*, even to repeat offenders: Peter asks Jesus, "How often will my brother" (or in my case, father) "sin against me, and I forgive him? As many as seven times?" (Matthew 18:21). I can almost picture ol' Pete's face, smug with the assurance of his own magnanimity, crumpling in disbelief at Jesus's reply of "I do not say to you seven times, but seventy-seven times" (Matthew 18:22). (Some translations even put that number at "seventy times seven.")

It all seems a bit excessive until we remember, yet again, that there is no bottom to the well of Christ's love and forgiveness for *our* sins. And when our own well has run dry, He invites us to drink deeply of His water of life, which never runs out.

The Transformative Power of the Gospel

Friends, when I tell you that as an adult, with a heart far from perfection but changed by God-given freedom from bitterness, I have witnessed moments of gentleness in my father—toward me, toward my children—moments I never got to experience as a child...I can only boast in the transformative power of the gospel that makes this possible. Even as someone with a bipolar diagnosis, my dad has grounded periods that include times of genuine connection I never felt as a little girl. To watch the patience with which he untangles his grandboys' shoelaces, when my childhood featured little of that forbearance, is doubly sweet. And to hear my mom describe the specific and insightful ways that he prays for each member of my family when he is calm and at peace with himself makes my throat close with emotion for the changes God has wrought through the years.

The Lord may yet heal my father of his affliction this side of heaven. I can't know for sure. But something that I do know? Because of my relationship with my dad—from a place of true empathy—I am able to pray for and grieve with other women who wrestle with hurtful family relationships. I am able to "weep with those who weep" (Romans 12:15). I can even exhort younger women with biblical truth that they might ignore if they didn't feel I'd "been there" too. I love Jon Acuff's take on offering our suffering for the benefit of others: "The scars you share become lighthouses for other people who are headed to the same rocks you hit."

Also, when I tell you that I'm a better mother for having clawed my way toward forgiveness through prayer, confession, weeping, ranting, failure, repentance, and, ultimately, a meek acceptance of God's gift of freedom from bondage to the sin of bitterness, I am encouraging you to look for ways in which this might be true for you too.

We Can't Afford Not to Forgive

If we harbor unforgiveness in our hearts toward *anyone*, the Matthew 6:15 passage from earlier in this chapter assures us that God will withhold forgiveness from us as well. And that should be enough to drive us to our knees, begging the Lord to replace our hearts of stone with hearts of flesh that beat with His love for mankind.

Because "mankind" includes those of the tiny (and teenaged) human variety. Forgiveness is not just for grownups. And we will be hypocrites of a deplorable degree if we insist that our children "be patient, bearing with one another in love" (Ephesians 4:2 NIV) while we protect our "right" to stay angry with them— or with our husband or our dad or that snarky lady on the internet.

Forgiveness can be excruciatingly hard. I will never deny that. But it certainly isn't bad. *Unforgiveness*, in fact, is the ultimate bad idea as it has the power to torpedo us in life-destroying ways:

1. Torpedo relationships. Proverbs 10:12 says, "Hatred stirs up strife, but love covers all offenses."

2. Hinder our prayer life. Psalm 66:18 says, "If I had cherished iniquity in my heart, the Lord would not have listened."

3. Inhibit healing. James 5:16 says, "Therefore, confess your sins to one another and pray for one another, that you may be healed."

4. Make us susceptible to the Enemy's attack. Ephesians 4:26-27 says, "Be angry and do not sin; do not let the sun go down on your anger, and give no opportunity to the devil."

5. Prevent us from seeing God's goodness in our lives. Hebrews 12:14 says, "Strive for peace with everyone, and for the holiness without which no one will see the Lord."

6. Block forgiveness of our sins. Matthew 6:15 says, "If you do not forgive others their trespasses, neither will your Father forgive your trespasses."

Unforgiveness rules us; forgiveness releases us. If we desire our prayers for patience and wisdom as a mother to reach God's ears, we must forgive. If we hope to model repentance and reconciliation, we must forgive. If we want to be forgiven by our children, we must forgive.

If your very insides are twisting in revolt against the notion of letting someone off scot-free without being able to guarantee consequences, I've been there. It wasn't until I replaced the offending person's image with my own that the truth of my double standard hit me like one of those Bugs Bunny slaps with a glove full of bricks. And if that weren't enough conviction already, Colossians

As the Lord has forgiven you, so you also must forgive.

COLOSSIANS 3:13

3:12-13 piles it on: "Put on then, as God's chosen ones, holy and beloved, compassionate hearts, kindness, humility, meekness, and patience, bearing with one another and, if one has a complaint against another, forgiving each other; as the Lord has forgiven you, so you also must forgive."

The verdict is in: Forgiveness isn't optional if we want to mother well and be effective, Spirit-filled Christians. Thankfully, we need only have a heart positioned toward Jesus, not a heart that never struggles with sin. Praise God that He gave us the perfect example of forgiveness in His Son, Jesus. May the knowledge that we've been forgiven much wrong by the only sinless and perfect One inspire us to extend the same gracious pardon (over and over again) to our children, husband, family, and the world.

WISDOM FROM THE TRENCHES

Ten years ago, I could not have written either of these past two chapters from the same posture of hope and forgiveness the Lord has now granted me. And I know so many of you are reading them from a place of tender skin, open wounds, and picked-at scabs rather than healed scars.

So I wanted to include some encouragement about the daily discipline of forgiveness from my own mother, Beth, who agreed to share her wisdom from the perspective of a wife to a bipolar man for over forty-five years. This is her advice, put into my words, shared with her blessing and prayer that it will bolster and embolden those whose struggle feels endless.

We have the power to bind and loose. "Truly, I say to you, whatever you bind on earth shall be bound in heaven, and whatever you loose on earth shall be loosed in heaven" (Matthew 18:18). Whether we're dealing with our swirling thoughts, our bitter fixations, our tense spines, or our angry tongues, as Christians, we do not have to be a slave to any of these things. And we don't have to hold others hostage to them either. We have the power, through Christ, to set ourselves (and others) free.

Scripture is essential. Some nights I lie awake, having made it through the day by the skin of my teeth, and ask the Lord for a verse, a phrase, or a memorized tidbit to usher me into sleep and give me supernatural strength for the next day full of struggle. He is faithful to answer with just what I need. But I have to be willing to fill my mind with His goodness and truth. I listen to Scripture as I fall asleep at night and in the car as I drive. I remind myself of it as I water my plants or wash my dishes. I read it every day in my Bible. It is one very tangible way that God is my "very present help in trouble" (Psalm 46:1).

We must guard our tongues. Proverbs 18:21 says, "Death and life are in the power of the tongue, and those who love it will eat its fruits." If we love death, we will speak it (and eat of its fruit). If we love life, we will speak it (and eat of its fruit). There's no way around it: If we want to truly live, we must choose to speak life or, at the very least, hold our tongues when we have nothing life-giving to say. (I sometimes fail to keep my tongue in check, so I should know.)

We must lose our life to gain it. "For whoever would save his life will lose it, but whoever loses his life for my sake will find it" (Matthew 16:26). Many would say I would have been better off leaving my husband long ago. But our allegiance as Christians is to God, not to what "many would say." God has shown me, through great personal hardship, what it looks like on a practical level to lose so much of what many consider a "normal" life in this world to gain everlasting life in Him. It's a painful process and often a lonely one. But He has never failed to show Himself faithful and good to me.

Confession is good for the soul. "Confess your sins to one another and pray for one another, that you may be healed" (James 5:16). The last thing you'll want to do is admit your wrongs to someone who is consistently wronging you. But the Bible says this is for *our* benefit and healing. And obedience to God's Word is better than clinging to "wronged party" status. What *they* do in return doesn't matter nearly so much as our willingness to do what God requires.

Entrust yourself to a just God. "When [Jesus] was reviled, he did not revile in return; when he suffered, he did not threaten, but continued entrusting himself to him who judges justly" (1 Peter 2:23). Jesus was vilified and mistreated, though He "knew no sin" (2 Corinthians 5:21). We can and should expect the same if we love the Lord. We also can trust and know that God is just and will never allow wrongdoing to go unpunished in the end.

Establish boundary lines. Jesus was no pushover. He rebuked Peter with "get behind me, Satan" because Peter's words were focused not "on the things of God, but on the things of man" (Matthew 16:23). He called the Pharisees out for their hypocrisy, overturned the money-changers' tables and drove them out with a whip, told the adulterous woman to "go and sin no more," and dismissed (with straight Scripture) Satan's attempts to woo him. Of course, we're not sinless like Jesus. But when it comes to living in a continually hard situation, calm, consistent, biblical boundaries for sanity, safety, and functionality are essential and even Christlike. The Lord will have to reveal what these should be in each specific scenario, but once He does, hold firm in the knowledge that God will be your just judge.

Trust in God for His peace. "You keep him in perfect peace whose mind is stayed on you, because he trusts in you" (Isaiah 26:3). It makes no earthly sense to experience God's peace when so much is beyond your physical control. But we always have the choice to turn our minds back to Christ and experience His peace "which surpasses all understanding" (Philippians 4:7). It's real. It's life-changing. It's not a crutch. It's essential to life, regardless of our circumstances.

Every bit of my mom's wisdom I've shared comes very much from "narrow road" principles (Matthew 7:13-14). Few have walked her path and stayed the course. Her choices make little sense to the world, which encourages us to abandon "stuck" situations when they no longer serve us or bring us joy. But this mindset is the "broad road" that is paved with self-justification, bitterness, divorce, broken homes, adultery, alcoholism, and so many more consequences of straying from the narrow path when circumstances feel unbearably hard. Having the privilege of watching my mom lean with all her might on Jesus my entire life has been one of the pillars of my faith. Her example of steadfastly blessing the name of the Lord in the face of genuine suffering inspires me daily to do the same in my own much less challenging circumstances. I pray that her faithfulness to God and to her family will inspire you too.

~ DAD THOUGHT ~

Mamas, there's one more hard-to-forgive person that Abbie didn't mention: you. (Sorry, dads. If you're anything like I am, you're already plenty good enough at forgiving yourself.)

Self-pardon is often harder for mothers than for fathers. That mama-bear nature that drives you to fiercely protect your children and desire the best for them can backfire when you know an oversight or a misstep or a downright sin has done your child harm.

I saw a video once where a bear was walking through the woods and came upon a mirror that had been set up in a stand at a trailhead. When the bear saw its own reflection, it ferociously attacked until the stand, mirror, and reflection were no longer a "threat." Mamas, can you picture yourself in that scene, seeing in that reflection some careless moment, harsh word, or error in judgment and then relentlessly beating yourself up about it?

The truth? It's impossible to parent perfectly for a single day, let alone for a child's life. Yet God's love covers a multitude of sins (1 Peter 4:8), including imperfect discipline, irritability, and laziness. Just repent and start again.

Remember: There ain't nobody that loves your babies more than their mama!

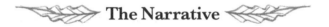 **The Narrative**

THE WORLD'S RESPONSE TO HARD	A CHRISTIAN RESPONSE TO HARD
Keeps a sliding scale of offenses	Knows that *all* have sinned and fallen short of God's glory
Considers forgiveness only from a human perspective	Sees the impact of forgiveness in light of what Christ did for us
Refuses to forgive if the recipient of the forgiveness is not "worthy"	Forgives because Christ first forgave us

Action Steps

- Memorize and meditate on Ephesians 4:32: "Be kind to one another, tenderhearted, forgiving one another, as God in Christ forgave you."
- Ask the Lord to reveal if there is someone that you subconsciously (or consciously) believe does not deserve your forgiveness.
- Have a conversation with a trusted older woman, your husband, or your accountability partner about the unforgiveness you feel (and why you feel it) and ask them to intercede for your heart to be softened and your perspective to be shifted toward that of Christ's example of ultimate sacrifice and forgiveness.

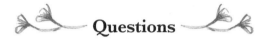

Questions

Why do we often tend to think of ourselves as easier to forgive or more deserving of forgiveness than those from whom we are withholding forgiveness?

What are some truths from Scripture that combat our desire to protect our right to "stay mad"?

Is there a time in your past when you were forgiven much by someone else? If so, how has that affected your life?

Prayer

Lord, You tell us in Your Word that whoever has been forgiven much loves much, but "whoever has been forgiven little loves little" (Luke 7:47 NIV). Soften our hearts to recognize just how much we have been forgiven and just how good it is to forgive others too (even though it's so hard!).

9

Hard Is Not the Same Thing as Good

IF IT'S NOT GOD'S WILL, IT'S JUST BAD

M ama, Jack's hurt!"

"What did you say, Honor?"

"It's Jack! Mama, he's hurt! And they're going to get him!"

"Who's going to get him?"

I stopped buttering Shiloh's toast mid-spread and hurried over to the dining room where several of my children were already huddled, noses pressed against the big bank of windows like the little smudge-making machines they are.

A Worrisome Situation

I searched our yard for signs of our lone male cat, Jack, until I spotted a blob of barely moving gray fur against the grass one hundred feet away. At first, it was hard to tell if it was, indeed, a creature of the feline persuasion, but the shape and size seemed right. What wasn't hard to determine was that, whatever it was, several large vultures had noticed it, too, and had decided it looked tasty. Soon, every member of our family was glued to the window (smudges be darned), watching in horror as the hulking monsters hopped with grotesque deliberation toward the prone animal.

I swiped my shirt sleeve across the fogged-up glass and realized, with a pang of dread, that it really was Jack.

"Move, buddy," I whispered. "Just get up and get yourself out of there."

Soon, the kids took up the chant: "Move, Jack! MOVE!"

He couldn't hear us, of course, but just as I began to think that I might need to have a throwdown with some really ugly birds to avoid my children witnessing a National Geographic episode in our front yard, a flicker of movement caught the corner of my eye. We swiveled in concert to stare as one of our female cats slunk along the edge of the yard toward the wooded section at its farthest border. When she reached it, she began working her way through the underbrush toward Jack. Only a few seconds passed before one of her sisters—then, moments after that, another—followed behind her, crouching low and moving with rolling, liquid shoulders and stealthy grace.

"Are they...rescuing him?" Della asked.

"Maybe," Shaun said. "But if that's it, why don't they just run at the birds to scare them away?"

Rescue Mission or...Breakfast?

Everyone fell silent again, and we held our collective breath as Jack's sisters participated in the strangest, most primal dance I have ever witnessed from a group of domesticated animals. It's a good thing the vultures were still too far away from Jack for us to truly worry, because we were all too transfixed by the other cats' stealth mission to tear our eyes away. Still, several of the younger kids were whimpering with worry for poor Jack, who hadn't managed to move beyond a twitch of his tail. Suddenly, Honor could stand it no longer, rushed to the front door, and beat his hands against the glass, shrieking, "*Run*, Jack, *run!*"

To our utter astonishment, Jack, who was now approached on three sides by leering death-birds, popped up and trotted nimbly toward the tree line to join his sisters, all three of whom watched with a distinct air of what can only be described as disappointment as the big birds launched themselves heavily into the air and flew away.

Shaun and I made shocked eye contact over the kids' heads as all four cats sauntered back the way they'd come, looking annoyed (except for Jack, who appeared downright chipper and relieved), and we said, practically in unison, "Were they *hunting* those vultures?!"

In a rush of giddy chatter, we all reached the same conclusion: Jack had been the bait (the downside of being the meek, lone male in a "pride" full of dominant sisters, apparently), and the ladies had been looking to bag something a little more exotic than Meow Mix for breakfast.

Recognizing When to Walk Away

I have been able to relate on a soul level to poor Jack's predicament at certain times and in certain relationships in my life. I don't have sisters to pressure me into "taking the fall for them," but just thinking of the lengths to which I have gone to avoid rocking the boat with a passive-aggressive friend or family member—not to please God but "man"—makes me wish I could reach through time, grab younger Abbie by her shoulders, give her a shake, and yell, "*Run!*" just like Honor did. Because there are certain hard situations the Lord calls us to bear (like a bipolar dad), but there are plenty of others that it would be wiser to escape altogether.

That first boyfriend—then fiancé—I mentioned a few chapters ago was a perfect example. He proposed on a snowcapped mountaintop during a church ski trip on the second anniversary of our first date. And I, a mere child of nineteen, said yes, not because my heart beat wildly with joy at the prospect of marrying him, but because I *knew*, the moment he dropped to one knee, that the rest of our group was waiting at the lodge to congratulate us, and I couldn't stand to disappoint everyone. I liked him a lot. He was one of my best friends. Everyone told us how well matched we were. I was resigned (my, what a romantic word) to the fact that we would marry *one day*.

But in that clutch moment when he proposed, my response told me everything I'd been unwilling to admit before. I wasn't ready for marriage. At least, not to him. The realization sat like an unexploded bomb in my chest on our ski down the mountain as the ragged edges of panic unraveled in my mind. I was engaged, and I wasn't even a little bit happy about it, which most people—me included—would consider a bad thing. I knew that feeling trapped, instead of ecstatic, right after someone slips a diamond solitaire on your ring finger was a big problem, but I was too "loyal" to do anything about it for another seven months. And even then the Lord had to orchestrate multiple circumstances that pushed me past my feelings of obligation and "stick with it even if it's not right" allegiance so I could summon the courage to break it off.

Maybe you've never been engaged to a guy you don't actually love, but I strongly suspect there are situations in your life that cause you to resonate with the "I'm here because I'm not supposed to run when the going gets tough, even when the tough is downright wrong" sentiment.

Hard Does Not Equal Righteous

Y'all, I may be the girl who's quick to remind you that "hard is not the same thing as bad" when you're convinced your preteen's emotional yo-yo tricks will be the demise of your sanity, but I am just as likely to be the girl who reminds you that hard is not the same thing as good either, when everything in your mama intuition tells you your daughter is in danger of burnout if she perseveres with the demanding club gymnastics schedule that's wrecking your family's peace and giving her panic attacks.

Just because something is challenging or hurtful or difficult does not mean that it possesses an inherently righteous quality or that we're "copping out" if we pivot when we feel convicted to do so.

Just because something is challenging or hurtful or difficult does not mean that it possesses an inherently righteous quality or that we're "copping out" if we pivot when we feel convicted to do so. That conviction may come in a realization that we are slogging through a needless hardship, like my self-inflicted, overstuffed Mondays. It may arrive in the timely words of a husband who recognizes the correlation between a poisonous friendship and our own increasing negativity. It may even show up in bouts of insomnia and anxiety.

The Lord may use any number of methods to nudge us and say, "Hey, beloved, this hard thing you're doing is outside My good and perfect will for you, and it's keeping you from Me and My purposes for your life."

Scripture makes it very clear that how we spend our time matters. And the people we allow to influence us in how we spend that time matter too. Ephesians 5:15-16 exhorts us to "look carefully then how you walk, not as unwise but as wise, making the best use of the time, because the days are evil." It does *not* tell us to say yes to every person who thinks we'd be great at leading worship while nursing a newborn, or that we should for sure oversee that new chapter of homeschool co-op because we have "such good leadership skills," or that starting a network marketing hustle would be a great idea in between therapy appointments for our dyslexic child.

There's nothing in the Beatitudes about "blessed are those who grit their teeth the hardest through the most frustrating or fruitless situations, for theirs is the biggest martyr trophy."

The Beatitudes passage does bless those who are poor in spirit, and those who mourn, and the peacemakers. All of those are incredibly hard things, but none of them stem from a refusal on our part to accept God's clear instructions to avoid them. On the contrary, the reward for enduring each of these hardships is, respectively, the kingdom of heaven, godly comfort, and being called God's children (Matthew 5:3-10). What incredible trade-offs!

There's No Such Thing as a Supermom

The tension comes in the discernment of whether a hard thing in our lives is primarily an opportunity for learning to persevere in right doing (think: the utter devastation of Job's life before God restores him), or for enduring the Lord's chastening (think: David's newborn son, conceived in adultery, dying soon after birth), or for promoting character building (hint: it pretty much always can be that last one).

Or if it stems from a stubborn refusal to acknowledge our own God-given limits.

My dear friend Kristy has the kind of gift for words that makes me want to snap my laptop shut, hand it to her, and say, "Here. You do it. I am not worthy." Years ago, when she and I first connected on the internet through the medium of blogging, she was teetering on the edge of a published book deal. For reasons I don't fully recall, it never came to fruition, but I gobbled up each blog post she wrote with eager anticipation for the day she would be able to place a book of her signature blend of lyricism and wit in my hands.

Almost a decade later, that day still has not arrived, in great part because Kristy recognized that at that time, the challenge of book writing while homeschooling her children, taking three of them to weekly therapy sessions related to learning disabilities, making food for a very strict diet aimed at improving their conditions, and serving her community as an army chaplain's wife was not making the best use of time and was depleting her reserves faster than she could replenish them.

Multiple years after each of her children graduated from therapy, Kristy, still unpublished but also still using her considerable talents, including writing, offered up her home to our family of twelve when we visited Alaska, where she serves with her husband (now a pastor) at their church. I was so blessed to get to observe the ways in which she prioritizes the many demands on her time. She models such a grace-filled and God-honoring balance of productivity and hospitality.

At one point, I walked into her kitchen to discover three big jars of kombucha lined up on her counter. I'll admit, my knee-jerk reaction was to think, "With everything she has going on, she still makes kombucha? I need to get my act together!" As if she could read my thoughts, she brought me back to center with one calm observation: "It's actually been a while since I've made kombucha because I only have so many things I'm capable of doing at once."

How much needless hardship, stress, and sorrow would we avoid in our lives if we all lived by this simple truth!

When we choose a path that would otherwise be an automatic no, and we say yes solely to avoid conflict or keep an unhealthy status quo, a warning signal should sound in our hearts.

Don't Be like Jack

Instead, all too often, we take the approach of Jack the cat and collapse under peer or family pressure to conform to their standards for our lives rather than God's. Do our family and friends often offer wise counsel? Of course! And when it is steeped in truth, we should listen well, "For by wise guidance you can wage your war, and in abundance of counselors there is victory" (Proverbs 24:6). But when we choose a path that would otherwise be an automatic no, and we say yes solely to avoid conflict or keep an unhealthy status quo, a warning signal should sound in our hearts. And when we withstand misguided attempts to compel us into a hard the Lord never intended for us, we experience freedom.

I'm reminded of Martha, toiling and perspiring in the kitchen, determined to make everything "just so," while Mary sat at the feet of Jesus, soaking in His words. Certainly, Martha's tasks were harder than her sister's that day, but they were not ultimately better. When Martha demands that Jesus send Mary in to help out with the chores, Jesus doesn't say, "You have chosen to muscle through the difficult stuff, which is always the right thing to do," but instead, "Martha, Martha, you are anxious and troubled about many things, but one thing is necessary. Mary has chosen the good portion, which will not be taken away from her" (Luke 10:41-42).

I strongly suspect that, in a culture in which women routinely tackled such physically strenuous tasks as hauling water from the well, scrubbing and beating out dirty clothes against stones, kneading and punching down the daily bread, preparing game for meals, sweeping the ever-present dust from the floors, and so much more, there was plenty of dirty, hard work to go around. No doubt, Mary did her fair share day in and day out. But she also displayed an admirable resistance to her sister's guilt trip in the presence of the Lord. By prioritizing time with Jesus, Mary demonstrated something that each of us would do well to learn: Hard work is good and necessary, and it will always be there for those who desire a home of peace and order. But we lighten that load when we choose to center ourselves in Christ first.

Only then are we able to approach our responsibilities with more joy, more energy, and more purpose than if we were to adopt Martha's response of fretting and frothing over every last thing on our endless to-do lists. Notice that Jesus does not criticize her work ethic but her attitude toward work. It is not ultimately the hardship, then, that is not good in this case, but the way in which our heart's focus is so easily drawn to the work rather than the Giver of it.

- Motherhood burnout is hard and not good.
- Doing everything ourselves without asking for help is hard and not good.

- Ignoring our emotions and pretending that everything is fine when we're drowning is hard and not good.

- Taking on too much in the name of "doing it all" is hard and not good.

- Starving ourselves of God's Word, sleep, good nutrition, and basic hygiene is hard and not good.

- Trying to keep everyone happy at once (as opposed to honoring God and tending to our families first) is hard and not good.

- Persevering in toxic, codependent mom friendships is hard and not good.

And yet, women tend to make excuses for why we "must" do each of these things because "that's motherhood."

"Can" and "Should" Are Not the Same

Such an attitude (which I have struggled with at times since becoming a mama) reveals a foundational lack of trust in God's ability to "supply all [our] needs according to His glorious riches in Christ Jesus" (Philippians 4:19 BSB). Though we might not actually *say* it, we think, "I mean, I know He's *capable*, but I'm not a quitter. I'll take His help as a last resort, thanks. I can push through."

Except "can" and "should" are two very different animals.

Hear me, friends: There is *absolutely* a biblical precedent for perseverance in the face of hard things. I couldn't write this book if there weren't. Romans 5:3-5 says, "Not only that, but we rejoice in our sufferings, knowing that suffering produces endurance, and endurance produces character, and character produces hope, and hope does not put us to shame, because God's love has been poured into our hearts through the Holy Spirit who has been given to us."

But there's also a biblical precedent for recognizing where true strength and wisdom come from.

Notice the progression of growth in the verses above: endurance to character, character to hope, hope to love. But notice also that this verse refers not to our tendency to plow through clear roadblocks in the name of survival but to

Suffering produces endurance,
and endurance produces character,
and character produces hope.

ROMANS 5:3-4

the kind of God-allowed and God-orchestrated hard scenarios that He sustains us through for our good and His glory. It ends with hope and God's love in our hearts, not exhaustion and depression.

The Trap of Bootstrap Motherhood

No matter what the world tells us, not all hard things in motherhood are inherently bad. But then again, neither are they all inherently good, no matter what our superhero complex would have us believe. Yes, we go through seasons of barely hanging on, when we can't imagine doing anything more than the bare minimum on three hours of sleep. And the good of those times is evident in how generous the Lord is to sustain us in our struggle and how much closer we can draw to Him in our oh-so-obvious time of need. But it's the moments when He gently nudges open the door to a new, kinder season—when the light spills in and we scrabble backward into the corner, clutching our overwhelm and squinting in distrust—that reveal the ways in which bootstrap motherhood keeps us from total dependence on Christ.

I love what Elisabeth Elliot says about Jesus's perfect surrender to the Father's will:

> He never made a fuss about anything. This spirit of peace can be in us who are *in Him*. We can learn to see every minute of our day as His, not ours; every task to which we turn our attention as belonging to Him, not to us, everything that interrupts 'our' work as His work which must take precedence. Knowing where we come from and to Whom we are going relieves us of the anxiety that makes us so fussy and so hard to live with.

If we ever convince ourselves that "I've got this" or even "I must do this alone," we are flirting with a hardship that only ends in hopelessness and strife. May we be ever mindful of the easy yoke and light burden that can be ours, even in the midst of challenges, when we prioritize God's will over self-sufficiency, when we recognize that doing more for its own sake is never a badge of righteousness and will only ever end in the kind of hard that hinders, not enhances, our work for the Lord.

DAD THOUGHT

Having grown up in the era of peak motivational poster popularity, I was bombarded with phrases like "You never fail until you stop trying," "There's no substitute for hard work," and "Quitting is for losers."

While these can be good motivational messages, without the proper guidance and direction behind them, they can also serve to magnify unhealthy male determination in areas where we already desire to excel:

- Tell us pain is gain, and we'll push through the burn to shave a second off our time.
- Tell us hard work pays off, and we'll put in the extra hours to climb the corporate ladder.
- Tell us practice makes perfect, and we'll change a thousand diapers to perfect our technique.

Waaait a second. One of these is not like the others.

And why is that? Because we've been wound up with motivation and let go without being taught biblical priorities to guide our energies. We have run afoul of the truth that "enthusiasm without knowledge is no good" (Proverbs 19:2 NLT).

Putting in overtime to excel at work is hard. Competing in a triathlon is hard. Earning the next degree is hard. Starting a side business is hard. All of these efforts *can* be worthwhile, but we shouldn't allow them to supplant the higher priorities of being an excellent disciple, husband, or father, lest we make life even harder for those we care about most.

I come from a long line of workaholics, so it is no surprise I found myself on the wrong side of that struggle early in my marriage when I made the leap to self-employment. I distinctly remember how stubbornly focused I was on accomplishing my goals, to the detriment of time with my wife and baby son.

It was Abbie's urging me to look up and look around at the needs of my family—to reprioritize—that helped me break away early from the examples of my dad and grandfather (both of whom came to this realization later in life).

Her frank encouragement, even though it rankled at the time, was a necessary wake-up call.

Do I sometimes still find myself lifting my head from my work only to realize lunch skipped by and it's time for dinner? Yes. I may never fully be rid of the tendency to overwork, but I am so grateful that I will *not* lift my head one day in the future only to discover my children flying the nest as I grasp at their tail feathers in an attempt to snatch back missed opportunities.

It's so much better to delay, or even never achieve, some monetary or other personal goal—which promises a fleeting reward that fades once attained—than to fail in our biblical responsibility to love and serve our God, our spouse, our children, and our neighbors, which promises a reward that multiplies in this life and lasts forever in the next.

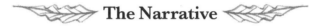 **The Narrative**

THE WORLD'S RESPONSE TO HARD	A CHRISTIAN RESPONSE TO HARD
Keeps the status quo, even when it's harmful	Is willing to reassess and change directions
Focuses on goals rather than God's will	Submits plans to God in an attitude of humility
Caves to peer pressure to perform	Stands strong in the knowledge that hard—simply for the sake of pleasing man—doesn't equal good

 **Action Steps**

- Write down one scenario in which the hardship you're experiencing is *not* a good thing.
- Ask the Lord to show you what about this situation is outside His will for your life.
- Commit to praying about and discussing with your husband (or, if no husband, someone trusted and godly) some alternatives or solutions to the "hard-and-bad" circumstance. As the Lord reveals solutions, step forward in faith to implement them, even if they feel hard too.

 **Questions**

What did God reveal to me about a "hard-and-bad" situation in which I find myself?

What are some good alternatives to continuing in this situation?

How can I avoid finding myself in similar scenarios in the future?

Prayer

Lord, we know that You give wisdom "generously to all without reproach" (James 1:5). Prod our hearts to boldly claim this truth when we find ourselves floundering in poor choices or harmful circumstances that seem beyond our control, knowing that they are never outside of Yours.

10

Finding Good Mom Friends Is Hard

MAKING THE EFFORT, ESTABLISHING HEALTHY BOUNDARIES, AND LEANING INTO CONNECTIONS THAT LAST

E very week, my inbox is bombarded by relationship queries just like these during my Whaddya Wanna Know Wednesday question and answer series:

- "How do you find your tribe?"
- "I'm so lonely. I keep reaching out and getting rejected. What am I doing wrong?"
- "I'm desperate for community. How did you build that kind of connection while still investing in your family?"

- "A longtime friend is ghosting all my texts. I don't know what happened. Any advice?"
- "When is it time to walk away from a toxic relationship?"

I could write an entire book about what the Bible says about healthy Christian relationships, but for now I'm choosing to devote a single chapter to both the pitfalls and joys of building godly "mom friendships" that can stand the test of even the most intense postpartum seasons or in-the-trenches stresses. I have been gifted with a few such relationships, and have endured the hurt of several more that floundered under the weight of jealousy and misunderstandings, and I can attest that both have the power to make us more like Jesus.

Kindred Spirits Are Worth the Effort

Of course, we all long for an instant "Anne and Diana" kindred spirit connection, but it's rare. Like-minded mamas with whom we effortlessly click sometimes feel as easy to find as a yeti, but unlike bigfoot, they do exist—and they're worth the hard work of making ourselves available in the midst of the busyness that motherhood brings. Because, unfortunately, initial friendship chemistry all too often fizzles when we're too occupied with potty training and carpooling to do what it takes to keep the spark alive.

I will talk more in a bit about the kinds of efforts that yield the biggest practical payoffs, but first I want to note this: We live in a world that glorifies instant gratification in every aspect of our lives—food, sex, money, attention, and, yes, friendship. According to tidbits of advice passed out on morning talk shows or in the glossy pages of women's magazines, if a girlfriend isn't your "ride-or-die" (if she won't follow you into and support you in any scenario), she's not worth the effort. And if it doesn't work out right away, it wasn't meant to be.

On top of that, worldly shows like *Keeping Up with the Kardashians*, *The Real Housewives* franchise, and *Sex and the City* (to name a few) paint a tumultuous and drama-filled picture of relationships that—while the perfect recipe for addicting television that appeals to our flesh—can have a warping effect on our view of true connection. They normalize and even glorify gossip, "venting" (really, petty complaining), harmful romantic entanglements, supporting a friend's choices, no matter how ungodly, and labeling any form of disagreement as "toxic."

A Biblical View of Friendship

It's enough to strip even the naivest among us of our altruism and coat our relational expectations with a veneer of cynicism. Thankfully, we have Scripture to refute the lies of secular culture and point us right back to the truth of what healthy, flourishing mom friendships should look like.

The world says, "Gossip is no big deal. Everybody does it."

The Bible says, "A perverse person stirs up conflict, and a gossip separates close friends" (Proverbs 16:28 NIV).

Also: "Whoever would foster love covers over an offense, but whoever repeats the matter separates close friends" (Proverbs 17:9 NIV).

The world says, "Being 'bad' is fun."

The Bible says, "Do not be misled: 'Bad company corrupts good character'" (1 Corinthians 15:33 NIV).

Also: "One who has unreliable friends soon comes to ruin, but there is a friend who sticks closer than a brother" (Proverbs 18:24 NIV).

The world says, "We deserve to vent without judgment."

The Bible says, "Therefore encourage one another and build one another up, just as you are doing" (1 Thessalonians 5:11).

Also: "Perfume and incense bring joy to the heart, and the pleasantness of a friend springs from their heartfelt advice" (Proverbs 27:9 NIV).

The world says, "Relationships should be perfectly equal."

The Bible says, "Be devoted to one another in love. Honor one another above yourselves" (Romans 12:10 NIV).

Also: "Do nothing out of selfish ambition or vain conceit. Rather, in humility value others above yourselves" (Philippians 2:3 NIV).

There are literally dozens more verses about what admirable conduct within friendship looks like, but all the examples I've given illustrate that, far from being a coincidence, solid friendships are the result of dogged effort, humility, and integrity. I can testify to this truth. My most cherished friendships have

Be devoted to
one another
in love.
Honor one
another above
yourselves.

ROMANS 12:10
(NIV)

developed slowly over time through perseverance and the kind of gradually budding connection that forges the steeliest bonds.

The Slow Road to Deep Connection

A perfect example of this is my dear friend Jennifer Flanders—whom I chose as the de facto editor for my books, even over the one my publisher offered me, both because of her grammar expertise and also because she just "gets" me. She's one of the greatest forces for good in my motherhood journey because of her incredible capacity for speaking words of unabashed positivity, encouragement, and practical advice over my parenting, my marriage, my writing, and my online ministry. I have extolled the virtues of my own mother many times on my social media and in my books. I could not have asked for a better one. But my mom's gifts primarily lie in the realm of showing, rather than telling. Her heart of service is beautiful, but to someone who also thrives on *words* and, more importantly, specific words of affirmation and exhortation, Jennifer's friendship has been invaluable.

Jennifer and I met at our homeschool co-op where we often sat side by side, grading feverishly so we wouldn't have to take any work home. We didn't have much time to talk, but we managed to fit in little spurts of conversation while our red pens flew. Year after year, we gravitated toward the same grading table, and our friendship outside of co-op gradually grew as well. Jennifer is seventeen years my senior, and she has twelve children, most of whom are much older than mine, but her youngest three match up perfectly in age and gender with my oldest three, Ezra, Simon, and Della. In fact, most of the times Jennifer and I were able to connect through longer conversations were as all ten of my kids, five or six of hers, and even a few of her grandchildren engaged in cherry-pit-spitting contests, dining table ping-pong, freeze tag in the yard, or rolling around on the rug at our feet.

Through the years, we have connected over similarities: blogging (you can find her at flandersfamily.info), big-family dynamics, DIY projects, and thrifting, to name a few. And we've also encouraged each other in our differences. She's impressed that I teach fitness classes and make time for ministry on social media. I'm in awe of her handicrafts and organizational skills. We've even bonded over that one time *20/20* came to her home to interview both of us (whom they found on the internet completely independently of each other, without any idea that we were real-life friends, if you can believe it) about our thoughts on "culture war" topics such as abortion (we're both staunchly pro-life) and gender identities (we both believe that God created only males and females and that He gave each person their sex with great intention and care). But that's another story for another book.

To say that she is my mentor would be accurate because I've learned so much from her, but she's never treated me as anything other than a trusted peer and one from whom she says she has learned as well. I prayed for years (over a decade) for a friendship full of Titus 2 wisdom and the kind of mutual respect and contribution that ours has. And I know how rare it is, both from my own experience and from the messages that flood my inbox, filled with longing for this very kinship.

We're Not Supposed to Have Twenty "Besties"

The truth is, with the demands of household and children and husbands, we're unlikely to have the margin to maintain more than one or two of these truly close-knit relationships at a time, so carrying an expectation of deep connection for every friendship just isn't realistic. My other "bosom friend" is the illustrator of this book, Lindsay Long, whom I've mentioned already (and whom I wrote about in more detail in the last chapter of *M Is for Mama*). Beyond that, I have my mom, my lovely sister-in-law, Hannah, and about a dozen other women I consider myself privileged to call close friends—Christlike, hardworking, joyful, inspiring, truth-loving mamas who are so faithful to "stir up one another to love and good works" (Hebrews 10:24).

For years, I didn't have those kinds of relationships, and now having such a deep pool of mama friends (of all ages) who love Jesus and others well is such a joy. But in most cases, I have to be content to enjoy their company periodically because none of us has the time to pursue anything further. Even for Jesus, with His twelve apostles, the Bible only describes one as the disciple "whom Jesus loved" (John 13:23). In fact, in that same passage, Peter leans over and nudges this disciple (most believe this is John who wrote Revelation) into asking Jesus a question, presumably because Peter believed Jesus would prioritize the beloved disciple's request. We don't know much else about their relationship from Scripture, but the implication is that this disciple invested in Jesus and held His confidence in a way the others did not.

I can't imagine what it would be like to be "besties" with God incarnate, but I am comforted that even Jesus had earthly limits to those who entered the inmost ring of His inner circle.

We Must Plant the Seed

Of course, this doesn't mean that we don't make efforts to include as many friends as possible in our sphere when the Lord drops opportunities for group gatherings in our laps. A few years ago, another mom from my homeschool co-op invited Della, Evy, and Nola to her house for a summer Bible study. It was only a few weeks long, but my girls enjoyed it so much that a tiny seed of an idea began to sprout in my mind. What if I were to invite certain capable moms to host a rotating schedule of get-togethers for our network of sweet daughter-friends? We could each choose the activity for our hosting day, provide a few snacks, and then sit and "visit" (as we Texans call it) while the girls chattered and played. The first two mamas I asked to cohost said yes, and, just like that, Grace Girls was born.

Little did I know that this simple idea would effortlessly blossom (truly, the easiest thing I have ever organized) into a full-fledged bimonthly meetup, complete with activities ranging from cake decorating and archery to shuffle dancing and scherenschnitte (a German cut-paper craft), and so much more. We now have up to fifteen moms who participate and as many as thirty girls—ages three through twenty—who attend. Most of the moms are at least a decade older than I am, but there are several who are younger as well, and the mix of ages, personalities, numbers of children, years of experience, and talents is my favorite!

Obviously, not every mom-friendship idea will work out as seamlessly as this one, but I do think this example illustrates something crucial to godly friendships: When God calls us to make the effort, we must obey. He alone can bring the harvest, but we must plant the seed.

Regardless of whether we achieve lifelong-friend status or simply enjoy friendship for a season, what should the guiding principles of godly mom friendships be? I asked Jennifer—whom so many call friend—for her best tips on the topic, and I've included them with mine (many of ours overlap), in no particular order, below:

1. Pray: Lift your friends up to the Lord (even before you have them).

2. Make the first move: Be willing to initiate (even after being rejected in the past).

3. Be hospitable: Open your home to others, whether you live in a mud hut or a mansion.

4. Skip comparison: With every mom you meet, there will always be something to make you feel "less than" or "more than," so don't even go there. It's not a competition.

5. Open your heart to service: Be willing to give and receive help.

6. Be honest: If you see a friend in error, or she approaches you for good advice, offer gentle correction in kindness and truth. (And be willing to accept the same from others!)

7. Be generous: Share your friends and introduce them to one another; don't be smothering or possessive.

8. Pursue genuine connection: We won't be bosom buddies with everyone, and that's fine. Some connections are stronger than others.

9. Practice humility: Steer clear of envy and cheer your friends on when they succeed.

10. Never gossip: Nothing kills a friendship more quickly than passing around "juicy morsels" behind someone's back.

11. Do it distracted: If we wait for the perfect time to get together, we may wait forever. Pursue the friendship, even if kids are underfoot and it's hard to finish a sentence.

12. Ditch toxicity: There's a place for acknowledging the hard and seeking help and encouragement. But there is no place for "husband bashing" or griping about our kids.

Flipping the Narrative for Good

Although I could add any number of things (Be considerate of different parenting styles! Don't forget about single moms! Be quick to overlook offense!), I want to address that last point specifically. We live in a culture that views mockery as an acceptable—celebrated, even!—form of social interaction. We scoff at the food other people eat, the clothes they wear, the number of children they have, the music they listen to. The list is endless, and sadly, this sneering attitude has slithered its way into even Christian homes and curled up right next to those we love most. If we, as followers of Jesus, desire to flip the narrative around husbands who are described as "another child" or kids who are "so annoying" (at best), we must be willing to draw a line in the sand with our girlfriends.

If we, as followers of Jesus, desire to flip the narrative around husbands who are described as "another child" or kids who are "so annoying" (at best), we must be willing to draw a line in the sand with our girlfriends.

My good friend Susan, a mama of nine who is equal parts feisty and sweet, does this so well. If a conversation even begins to veer toward snark about husbands or characterizing kids as burdens, she speaks up immediately with calm, loving conviction. She doesn't just change the subject. Instead, she puts it plainly: "Ladies, this is not God-honoring, and it's unfair to our families. We need to guard our tongues diligently and not give Satan an opportunity." I love her for her boldness and commitment to holding her friends to a high standard of holiness, even in the face of potential backlash.

When It's Just Not Working

So what do we do when the backlash inevitably comes, perhaps even in cases when we have done nothing wrong? Our list above, while steeped in biblical principles, assumes goodwill on the parts of both participants in the relationship, but that's not always the case. Unfortunately, we women can be so desperate for connection that we overlook clear warning signs of dysfunction in favor of clinging to a "friendship" that is anything but friendly. And I know this because I have been there on two separate occasions in my life. And in both cases, the other women involved were Christians.

In neither case did the relationship end well, and a great deal of that had to do with my people-pleasing tendencies that allowed habitually harmful behaviors to go unaddressed in the name of "peace." After all, Romans 12:18 exhorts us to "live peaceably with all." So that means I have to be friends with everybody, right? Wrong. If we only look at the second half of the verse, we will completely miss the crucial context of the first half: "If possible, so far as it depends on you."

Did a lightbulb just click on in your brain too? Yes, we are commanded to love our neighbor as ourselves, and Jesus makes it very clear in the parable of the Good Samaritan that the term "neighbor" includes even those whom the world tells us we "should" despise. But there are situations in which we will not be mutually at peace with certain people, and it's because they are withholding their peace from us.

Hear me: *Inasmuch as we are able to contribute to the peace, we do.* And we must be honest about and repent of the times we have contributed to strife instead.

But I'm guessing we can all remember occasions as teenagers when our mom dropped us off for a sleepover, and we ended up sitting on the bed swinging our legs awkwardly as our "friend" cleaned her bathroom and ignored us because she was already in a tiff over something unrelated to us when we got there. *That is withholding peace.*

Or maybe you too have found yourself tiptoeing around certain topics that should be benign but instead sit like powder kegs between you and a friend who is clearly offended by something you have done but refuses to address the emotional elephant in the room. *That is withholding peace.*

If the other party in the relationship consistently rejects our efforts for reconciliation or refuses to recognize the ways in which she is creating conflict, then continuing to invite that person into the softest places of our hearts is foolish. I can't tell you how many times, as a child and teen, I heard my mom exhort me to be "wise as serpents, and harmless as doves" (Matthew 10:16 KJV) in my dealings with others.

> *If the other party in the relationship consistently rejects our efforts for reconciliation or refuses to recognize the ways in which she is creating conflict, then continuing to invite that person into the softest places of our hearts is foolish.*

In other words, we strive to contribute only good while acknowledging that discernment is necessary when choosing those whom we fully trust. Establishing healthy boundaries may feel too difficult in the midst of a passive-aggressive attachment, but it's much easier in the long run than continuing in a bond of friendship to someone who might not even like us, much less truly love us.

In fact, the entire first half of Matthew 10 is devoted to Jesus instructing His disciples on how to do the hard work of evangelism in unknown territories.

"Whatever town or village you enter, search there for some worthy person and stay at their house until you leave...If the home is deserving, let your peace rest on it; if it is not, let your peace return to you" (Matthew 10:11-13 NIV). I know this is a passage about preaching the gospel, but I can't help but see some correlations to how we should approach any relationship:

1. Pursue friendship with those whom the Lord places in our path.

2. Offer our peace. If they are deserving of it (the Greek word for "deserving" here is *axios*, which carries the connotation of "worthy" or even "suitable"), they will respond in kind.

3. If they are not deserving, retract our peace and continue on in search of softer hearts.

I cannot emphasize enough that this does not mean we shun anyone. Or that we won't have to work harder for some relationships than others. It simply serves as a guide for those to whom we offer true intimacy.

Pain Can Be a Good Teacher

In the first chapter of this book, I referenced a devastating friendship loss that I—and by extension, our whole family—suffered. The friendship arc was fraught with "envy and selfish ambition" (James 3:16 NIV) on both our parts. When I hold that relationship up to the light of the list Jennifer and I wrote (see page 144), I see glaring gaps in multiple areas relating to competition, humility, and celebrating each other. Also, I endured several months-long "freeze-out" sessions throughout our lengthy friendship, but I was never able to do more than guess at the reasons for them, because I always steered clear of confrontation and clarity in the interest of "not making her mad" (this phrase alone is a red flag).

Without the family connection, I think I would have drawn healthier lines sooner, after having dealt with a very similar hot/cold dynamic in my teens and early twenties. And it might have spared my heart much pain. But it's especially hard to maintain space when husbands and kids are involved. Also, not every aspect of the friendship *was* negative. We enjoyed each other's company much of the time, and we were able to support each other in practical ways throughout our pregnancies. But the off-balance feeling of never knowing where I stood kept me on edge, constantly wondering whether I had shared too much or done too little.

The Lord is able to use anything as an opportunity to magnify and reveal our sin to us so that we can learn to forsake it, and this relationship did just that for me—showing me propensities for jealousy and competition that I hadn't encountered in any other relationship. God forced me, through episodes of hurt feelings and offenses I took too much to heart, to answer some gut-wrenching questions about my own motivations. I didn't always like what I discovered in my heart. Thankfully, the Lord is also faithful to grow us in maturity as He peels the veil of self-deceit from our eyes. I learned so much, both about the sin that crouches at the door of my heart, eager to control me, and about what it meant to be its master in Christ's strength (Genesis 4:7).

The practical application of this (work-in-progress) mastery took several forms:

1. I stopped paying attention to anything this friend did that didn't materially affect me: vacations, online posts, parenting choices, whatever. If it wasn't something that directly involved me, I sought to release it to the Lord, or I literally limited my access to even knowing about it. After all, if her husband was on board with it, who was I to impose my own preferences or judgment on issues that were matters of personal choice rather than clear biblical instruction?

2. I started praying for issues that concerned me because she was my friend, instead of because I *wanted* to be "concerned."

3. I branched out into other friendships I had previously felt hamstrung to pursue because of the unhealthy, exclusive nature of our attachment.

These three choices released me from so much tension and mental gymnastics. But they weren't enough to prepare me for the implosion of the friendship several years later, the finale of which was an email detailing my shortcomings (perceived or real) and a complete dissolution of the relationship.

Beauty from Ashes

For several years afterward, I struggled with anxiety and self-doubt (the kind that had me peeking around the corners of grocery store aisles lest I run into her unexpectedly). But I was also able to take a long look at some of the accusations she had made, line them up against Scripture, and ask the Lord to "see if there be any wicked way in me" (Psalm 139:24 KJV). Of course, the answer, in some cases, was yes. It was a genuine struggle to separate the truth of my sinful tendencies from the lies of a skewed lens.

Praise God that He saw fit to give me friends like Jennifer and Lindsay, who quickly recognize when my thoughts are spiraling toward ungodly condemnation and who lovingly point me back to the truth of Christ's finished work on the cross for my sins. They have also shown me what it looks like to "do life" with women who check every last item on that "godly friend" list from above. In fact, I now credit the death of that one relationship with the health of at least a dozen others that I wouldn't have been emotionally available enough to nurture.

Through these friendships, I have experienced the truth of Isaiah 61:1-3 (NIV) in such a tangible way—"a crown of beauty instead of ashes, the oil of joy instead of mourning, and a garment of praise instead of a spirit of despair."

No heartache is wasted when we faithfully lay it at the foot of the cross.

It might be tempting to say, "Good riddance!" or, "That should have ended a long time ago." But the truth is that I'm a much better friend for having weathered less-than-ideal relationships. No heartache is wasted when we faithfully lay it at the foot of the cross. And even the heart-shredding endings don't have to stay painful forever. I only read the "all the things wrong with you" email once, but many years later I can still quote verbatim the harshest portions of it; *that* is how much power our words hold. About a year later, the Lord nudged me to write a letter confessing the ways I had sinned in our relationship and asking for forgiveness (I never heard back). He also eventually gave me the strength to invite her to lunch (I had to push through near-panic at the thought of seeing her again, but if you recall from when I mentioned this before, she came, and it was pleasant). Since then, we've had several brief-but-cordial interactions. Both acts of obedience helped provide a piece of the closure puzzle and set me free from an unreasonable worry about her opinion of me. Both were necessary, whether or not she ever responded.

Making godly mom connections is hard, friends. I know. It's only in my thirties and early forties, after years of learning from mistakes, after decades of consistent prayer and investment, that I have experienced the joy of lasting, mutually uplifting, and edifying relationships with other imperfect women who run hard after Jesus and encourage others to do the same.

If you're still entangled in a hurtful relationship or trudging through the desert of loneliness, I challenge you to ask the Lord not "Why are You doing this to me?" but "What are You teaching me in this?" The answer might just be what prepares you to be the best friend a girl could ask for.

Mamas, when it comes to social interaction, you might find that your husband tends toward one of two extremes. He either avoids social interaction like the uncomfortable, complicated mess it can be, or jumps at every chance to stick you with the kids while he heads out to play cards with his buds.

Both are forms of escapism. In the second example, he's using relationships as an excuse to avoid the hard prospect of finishing one job for the day only to come home and engage in another. But in the first example, he's fleeing the hard job of opening up and developing strong relationships.

If your husband tends toward the first, then when a like-minded and God-seeking (and therefore God-sent) friend materializes, encourage him to engage in more than superficial chatting at church. Ideally, they'll be able to meet at a time that doesn't add to your load, but even if a solo-parenting sacrifice is occasionally required, know that you're investing in spiritual growth, which will pay dividends in your marriage and parenting.

I have certainly benefited from Abbie's willingness to hold down the fort while I invest in mutually edifying relationships. She was even gracious enough to solo-parent for ten days—not once, but twice!—so I could take an epic male-bonding wilderness trip with my dad, brother, and older sons. (And husbands, this goes both ways. I also solo-parent a few times a year so Abbie can take time to rest or build a relationship—your wife needs it too!)

If your husband is the social grasshopper, ready to jump into any social opportunity at the slightest threat of child-rearing, he may also need encouragement to engage more deeply in a friendship.

Wait, what?

Yes, you heard me right. He likely needs a wise mentor (as opposed to just another Monday Night Football buddy). I can't overstate the value of the perspective of someone who has been there and is now willing to invest in a younger dad.

And if you are that grasshopper husband reading these words because your wife, who is drowning in diapers and dishes, handed you a book and said, "THIS!" I would encourage you to commit to consistently spending time with the Friend who created you—before you head off with your buds again. Your other friendships (including the one with your wife) will ultimately thank you for it.

 **The Narrative**

THE WORLD'S RESPONSE TO HARD	A CHRISTIAN RESPONSE TO HARD
Primarily seeks validation in friendship	Seeks to give and get encouragement and edification within friendship
Engages in complaining, venting, mockery, and gossip	Looks to sharpen and uplift, not gripe and tear down
Makes the friendship about self	Keeps the friendship about others first

 **Action Steps**

- Memorize and meditate on Hebrews 10:24-25: "And let us consider how to stir up one another to love and good works, not neglecting to meet together, as is the habit of some, but encouraging one another, and all the more as you see the Day drawing near."

- Make a list of one to three friends who exemplify the friend who loves at all times, (Proverbs 17:17) and then take a moment to encourage them in some way (text, voice memo, note).

- Write down a few names that come to mind when you think of difficult friendships. Take a moment to pray for each person by name (and don't just pray for them to "do better!").

- Ask the Lord to show you ways that you can be a friend to the friendless and a mentor to younger women in Christ. We are called to serve, not simply to be served.

Questions

How have good friendships made you a better Christian? How have hard ones done the same?

What are some concrete ways to invest in godly friendships in a busy season of motherhood, even if you don't yet have the friends you'd like?

Why do you think even some Christian friendships falter?

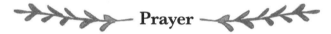

Prayer

Lord, You are the Friend who never fails, never backstabs, never flakes out on us. Thank You for Your example of self-sacrificing love. Give us a desire to "cover a multitude of sin" in our own relationships, knowing that we sin too and that God-given friendships are one of the best ways to enjoy motherhood in community with like-minded sisters in Christ.

11

Prioritizing Marriage Is Hard

PRACTICAL WAYS TO CHOOSE OUR SPOUSE EVEN WITH KIDS IN THE HOUSE

I almost broke up with my husband on our fourth date. We'd been email flirting for weeks—the kind of nerdy references and properly punctuated inside jokes that made my grammar-loving little heart thrill at the prospect of a handsome *and* wordy man.

Our first date was lovely and creative (I had to unravel a riddle to discover where to meet him for dinner). On the second one, I informed him I felt called to leave the ultimate number of kids I would have up to the Lord (because I was determined to run him off if he was run-offable), and he didn't even bat an eyelash. Good so far! On the third date, he came to my family's house for his birthday, and I made him a cheesecake (anybody who's ever made one knows this is a big commitment for a third date). On the fourth, I met *his* family, and then we went to our church's young-singles Super Bowl party together.

Oh, and did I mention these all took place one after the other over the span of four days? Yep, it was intense from the start with us.

Which is why I decided, on the way to the Super Bowl viewing, that I needed to walk away before things got too serious and my heart couldn't extricate itself from an attachment that was careening a bit too quickly from "like" toward "love" for my taste.

Too Nice or Just Right?

But, Abbie, why would you do that? If he was so great, why would you *want* to leave?

Because he was too nice.

Yes, you read that right.

I'm a strong personality, and as Shaun and I chatted and laughed, stayed up until 2:00 a.m. delving into important-to-us topics, and fell more and more "in like," I started to panic that I would be the bulldozer in the relationship. Now that we've been married for almost twenty years, he's told me multiple times how he admires my ability to quickly come up with a fully articulated response to questions. It takes him a bit longer to decide where he lands on an issue, and though I now respect his reticence to speak until he knows his own mind, back then, as a feisty twenty-one-year-old, I took his hesitation as a sign that he might just be a teensy bit of a pushover.

I don't know why I thought it would be a good idea to break up with a guy and then go watch the Super Bowl with a bunch of other people, but before I knew it, we were sitting in his Toyota Corolla outside the host's house, and I was stumbling through an awkward speech that started with "It's not you, it's me… because I can be kind of forceful, and you're *really* nice, but…"

Before I could complete that sentence, he turned toward me, looked me dead in the eyes, and said, "Listen, I really like you, but I'll be fine if this doesn't work out. I really think it could though. You're not the only one with opinions, and when I want to express mine, I'll speak my mind."

I just sat there blinking at him, pondering whether this was the single sexiest speech I had ever heard in my life. It didn't take me long to decide that it absolutely was. And I have never doubted my husband's confidence since that day (partially, I think, because my being honest with him let him know how important it was to me that he show it).

What I have doubted, though?

My own ability to maintain that same fluttery feeling in the pit of my stomach through the demands of one, then two, then three, then *five*, then six, then seven, then eight, then *ten* mouths to feed, bottoms to wipe (well, not all at once), brains to fill with knowledge, hearts to shepherd, and bodies to transport from point A to point B.

Rear Swats > Shakespeare

The answer, of course, is that I can't maintain it all the time, every day. If the success of my marriage were based on the number of newly-dating-level butterflies I feel toward my husband on a daily basis, it would look like a complete failure. But if it can be gauged by the number of times our eyes meet with happy crinkles in their corners over the tops of our twin toddlers' heads when they tumble into bed with us in the morning, or the instances when we wordlessly take a child from the other's arms because one of us is done eating and notices the other is not, or the moments when a playful swat on the rear or a hand rested at the small of a back speaks more loudly than any Shakespearean declaration of adoration ever could, then we might be all right.

Regardless of the number of kids, having children changes a marriage. Notice I did not say "weakens" or "worsens." I am convinced, from years of personal experience, from observing other families I admire, and from reading the Bible that having children enhances the marriage relationship—but only if we choose to prioritize our wedding vows above the demands of bath time and bickering, spilled breakfast and spiteful attitudes (ours and the kids').

I am convinced, from years of personal experience, from observing other families I admire, and from reading the Bible that having children enhances the marriage relationship—but only if we choose to prioritize our wedding vows above the demands of bath time and bickering, spilled breakfast and spiteful attitudes (ours and the kids').

It takes sacrifice, humility, and focused effort.

I do not find Shaun hard to love. He is kind, considerate, funny, intelligent, handsome, hardworking, involved, and about forty-seven more excellent adjectives that I'll spare you from reading for the sake of lowering our rating on the schmoopometer a bit. But I do struggle with prioritizing his wishes and preferences when I'm such a busy mama who already has the details of "my day" racing through my brain by the time my feet hit the floor in the morning.

Giving Preference to the Other

Chances are a fair number of you bristled at even the suggestion that our husbands' preferences should take precedence over our own, but Paul, in his Holy Spirit–inspired writings in Ephesians, is crystal clear in his exhortation that wives are to "submit to your own husbands, as to the Lord. For the husband is the head of the wife even as Christ is the head of the church, his body, and is himself its Savior. Now as the church submits to Christ, so also wives should submit in everything to their husbands" (Ephesians 5:22-24).

Now, I'm aware that biblical submission is hotly debated in Christian circles, and I don't have enough time in one chapter to do a deep dive into the whys and the wherefores of its truths. But I will say this: I have never found a woman who wants to write off biblical submission for wives (which is expressed succinctly in three verses) as a "cultural thing" or an example of "Pauline misogyny" who is equally eager to skip over his nine-verse dissertation on husbands' responsibility to "love your wives, as Christ loved the church and gave himself up for her" (Ephesians 5:25-33).

No, that part gets a standing ovation. Which means we might have some heart searching to do if we claim to love Christ and His holy Word, the Bible (especially when it tells our husbands to be nice to us), yet have a problem with submission.

I don't know about you, but I'm not prone to give my children instructions they don't need. I'm not known for saying, "Kids, make sure you eat *all* the chocolate chip cookies, okay?" or "Be sure to finish that movie you're watching!"

Why? Because kids need no encouragement to indulge in yummy treats and screen time.

Instead, I find myself needing to remind them multiple times a day to "be diligent in your work," "be considerate of others," "simmer down," or "listen up."

Adults are no different. When Paul instructs us women to put ourselves under our husbands' authority, it is both because it's an exemplification of the gospel and God's order in creation and also because we women can often become so used to managing *our* homes, *our* time, *our* children, that, far from checking in to make sure we're on the same page with our husband and hearing his wishes before independently forming our own, we feel affronted when he has the audacity to pencil anything into our carefully planned household playbook.

Conversely, men are often content to coast emotionally. Unless they feel urged to the contrary, some (not all) are quick to make a beeline for the remote and bypass an opportunity to stop and really listen (arguably one of the most loving things a man can do for a woman) as their wife recounts her hectic day of potty training, answering emails, and battling preteen sass.

Paul recognized these sinful tendencies within marriage and spoke truth that no doubt ruffled feathers in the first century as well. (Because if women were already submitting happily, and men were already loving their wives well, he might not have needed to address either issue.)

Purposefulness > Laziness

I'm writing this book primarily to women (although I regularly hear from mamas whose husbands have read portions of my book as well; my goal is always to speak to biblical *principles* rather than strictly "women's issues"). But I will say this to both the husband and the wife in a marriage: The solution to both misplaced authority and unloving behavior—besides repenting of sin!—is intentionality.

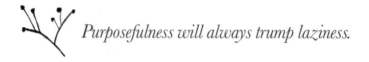 *Purposefulness will always trump laziness.*

Purposefulness will always trump laziness in marriage (in anything, really), but what does that look like on a practical level?

One simple way to be intentional in our marriages is to make a point of sitting down with our husbands to ask them in which areas they would like to have input before we proceed. Grocery shopping? Work hours? School choices? Potty training? The answer will be different for every marriage. (And if you've already made a habit of "doing your own thing" separately, the answer may initially be a blank stare.)

I know of men who want to be kept abreast of each of these areas (and more) down to the specific clothing bought for each child. I know of others who take a completely hands-off approach and wonder why their wives even bother them with questions about "the kids." There is potential for pitfalls in both extremes, but most men are pleased to know their wives respect and honor their leadership and wisdom enough to come to them first with household decisions.

At this point, Shaun leaves grocery shopping, homeschooling (including curricula purchases), kids' wardrobes, meal planning, maintaining the house, and coordinating the details of our day-to-day schedules to me. We've had multiple conversations about each of these areas in the past, and he has confidence that I will come to him with questions or concerns when I have them. And I do!

When our piano teacher offered our twin girls an hour-long lesson because they were advancing too quickly for the half-hour model, I was initially reluctant for scheduling and financial reasons. When I asked Shaun his opinion, he said, "Go for it! It'll be good for them." And so we did. And it's been such a blessing to our girls.

When I waffled for months about whether to continue attending two homeschool co-ops or to pare down to one, it was Shaun who (after giving feedback each time I brought it up) finally said, "The kids will be fine with one, and it'll be better for our family dynamic to have that extra day at home." And he was right!

Studying the Way Our Husband's Heart Beats

Proverbs 31:11-12 describes the goal for Christian wives and mamas: "The heart of her husband trusts in her, and he will have no lack of gain. She does him good, and not harm, all the days of her life." Building the kind of husbandly confidence that fosters true connection and trust within marriage requires a daily willingness to be flexible, humble, and servant-hearted (Ephesians 6:7). To listen with a teachable heart, even when he speaks into areas we think we've got locked down. To take an attitude of Christlike meekness (Matthew 11:29) instead of adopting a spirit of offense.

It's *hard*. There's no way around it. But like so many other difficult things, the more we practice and pray for God's strength to enable us, the more natural (and, hopefully, easier!) it becomes.

 It's impossible to discover ways in which we can best steward our husband's trusting heart if we don't invest the time to study the way it beats.

Of course, it's impossible to discover ways in which each of us can best steward our husband's trusting heart if we don't invest the time to study the way it

She does him good,
and not harm,
all the days of her life.
PROVERBS 31:12

beats. Sure, we used to be intimately acquainted with all his preferences and desires. As a girlfriend, fiancée, or young wife, we pay close attention to everything he likes, determined to be the greatest living expert on the man we love. But as the newlywed phase melts into sleepless nights with a baby, then a toddler, then job changes and night shifts, extracurriculars and money stresses, devoting time to relearning the particulars of our spouse feels less and less crucial to our daily survival.

It is from this place of "barely squeaking by" that so many touched-out, overstimulated, and exhausted mamas message me with questions about spending quality time together, finding time for sex, and figuring out how to even care enough to make an effort.

I get it.

I have experienced postpartum seasons of hormonal imbalances that left me with meager libido. I know what it's like to shrug Shaun's hand off my shoulder because I already felt like I was about to jump out of my own skin after being touched all day by small humans. I am familiar with mood swings, with times of emotional blankness, irritability, and the kind of sleep deprivation that feels like it really might kill you.

It would be so easy, especially as moms of young children, to say that the demands on our time and bodies are too overwhelming to allow space for pursuing our marriages, so they'll just have to wait until we get back to "normal."

Finding a New Normal

The problem? "Normal" is subjective, and we may never "get back there" (or discover a new version that benefits our marriage) without an active commitment to find workable solutions and pockets of time and energy that we can use as building blocks for better habits that will serve our marriages, and by extension our families, well.

There are obviously factors we cannot control, but we too frequently neglect the hard work of taking baby steps toward simple, repetitive improvements in the factors we *can* influence. And our entire household suffers as a result. We tell ourselves we couldn't possibly make time to sit down with our husband in the newborn season and actually stay awake long enough to carry on a conversation. Or we insist that since bedtime with three littles takes two hours, there simply won't be enough energy left for physical intimacy. Or we point out that, when we have teenagers awake and staring us in the face at 11:00 p.m., all hope of "us time" is gone.

The common denominator in each of these claims is an attitude of victimhood ("the kids make it impossible to…") rather than a proactive determination to prioritize our marriages by finding routines that restore margin to our overwhelm. I don't believe in a prescriptive approach to parenting because I know, from experience and observation, that it's possible to apply godly principles in a variety of successful ways that allow for different temperaments, preferences, and circumstances.

However.

If the problem is lack of sleep in the newborn stage or a protracted bedtime routine or teens who never seem to want to go to bed or (insert any other child-related obstacle to prioritizing marriage), then we must be willing to *do something about it*—other than throwing up our hands in despair.

All too often, marriage advice consists of "Date your spouse" and "Have sex regularly," which are both great tips. But it doesn't include a game plan for *how* to do either when we lack money for a babysitter or there's an infant sleeping in our room every night.

When I polled my readers for marriage connection ideas, the above two topics came up frequently, but so did strong pushback from some moms who feel bullied into striving for something they consider unattainable.

As a mama to ten children in fourteen years—including two sets of twins—I'm here to say it *is* possible to make both of these suggestions a habit *if* you're willing to (a) think of them as important elements of a thriving union (instead of something that would be "nice to do if XYZ would just fall into place") and (b) pursue them in creative ways.

Creativity, the Spice of Marriage

Shaun and I have had a once-a-week "date night" our entire marriage. But that doesn't mean we've always gotten dressed up, paid a babysitter, and eaten at a sit-down restaurant. In fact, until we had kids old enough to responsibly stay home with younger siblings, it was very rarely any of those things. Which means, for thirteen years, our date nights almost always consisted of an evening each week (typically on Thursdays) that we planned ahead to have kids in bed an hour earlier than usual so we could eat either takeout or something simple and yummy (like charcuterie-style finger food) and then snuggle and watch a movie, make out on the couch, play a board game, answer questions from one of those silly "couples quizzes" online, or simply hold hands and talk.

The focus? Uninterrupted time together and physical touch. Did it always end in sex? No, but the chances were strong, since we went to bed feeling more connected and relaxed than we had any other night that week. For us, it was less about the modern definition of a "date" and more about the intentionality of connection and building anticipation for what quickly became our favorite weeknight. And the fact that we had to work extra hard to "earn" it by planning ahead for both our tasks and the kids' bedtime routines only sweetened the payoff of sinking onto the couch together with a fist bump of congratulations when the littles were all in bed.

I'm aware not everyone's schedule allows for this level of regularity in the evenings. Maybe your "date" could be an early morning prayer time over coffee, a once-a-month picnic lunch while the kids run and play in the park, or a Saturday afternoon bedroom tryst while the littles nap. Maybe you despise the term "date." That's fine. It's just easier to say than "time of focused connection," which is the whole point.

The Nitty Gritty

Let me say this: Thursday night would have been much harder for me to pull off without consistent efforts toward routine in our home the other six days of the week. Again, these are not prescriptive, but because I am so often asked *how* I actually manage to enjoy my marriage (and I *really do* enjoy it so much!) without feeling completely dominated by our kids' schedules, I decided to include this list.

We sleep train our babies. I started out strict and have loosened up considerably with each baby. All have been sleeping solidly by the time they are a year old, though, and in focusing on getting our babies on a good "eat, play, sleep" rhythm during the day, and then working proactively to lengthen their sleeping stretches at night when they were ready, I gave myself some space to mentally breathe—and get some rest!

I take naps. I know this is not everyone's cup of tea, but I love a good power nap of twenty to thirty minutes, especially when I'm in the trenches with very young children (which has been pretty much my entire marriage). When do I do this? When my older kids have quiet time and my babies and toddlers take naps (which they regularly do at the same time because of the aforementioned effort to get them in a consistent sleep rhythm). Bonus for both me and Shaun: My naps are often the difference between "I have zero energy tonight" and "Hubba-hubba!" Note: I don't nap often when I don't have small babies, but it helps immensely in that season.

I exercise regularly. This may sound irrelevant to prioritizing my marriage. But numerous studies conclude that those who consistently move their bodies have more energy, lower stress, and an increased sex drive. Or as Proverbs 31:17 puts it: "She dresses herself with strength and makes her arms strong." I didn't know I was making an investment in my marriage when I became a fitness instructor over sixteen years ago, but all my efforts to exercise regularly have been paid back in full *with interest* (yes, even despite the car rides where we practiced our "screaming tolerance" with the twinsies)!

We keep bedtime routines simple. People regularly assume that, with ten offspring, bedtime must be a circus. But it's not. Was it when we only had very small children? Sure, at times. But that's why it's so important to remain dogged in a commitment to creating peaceful rhythms in our homes. They build upon themselves until we reach the point of being able to say, "Do your bedtime routines," and that's exactly what everybody does. For us, this only works if we keep things uncomplicated and brief. We brush teeth, go potty, get water, give hugs and kisses, and then go to bed. As a homeschool family, we will have already read and prayed together multiple times throughout the day, often including right before bedtime routines, so that is not an integral part of our sleep ritual.

We establish boundaries. Whether this means taking the date night *out* of the house now that we have older kids who don't go to bed early, setting aside Sundays as "everybody but Mama and Daddy is in bed by 8:30" nights, or nixing the bedtime "I forgot water! potty! kiss!" whack-a-mole (I talk about how we do this in *M Is for Mama*), drawing boundary lines around our time as a couple is key to actually enjoying it. Will there be seasons when the baby wakes up, the three-year-old is struggling with night terrors, or the preteen just needs some extra, focused attention with Mom and Dad? Of course. But the goal is to achieve consistency, not "perfection."

 The goal is to achieve consistency, not "perfection."

Prayer Is like Marriage Glue

There are so many other ways to keep our marriages at the forefront of our home life (leaving love notes on the bathroom mirror, sending spicy texts, random acts of sweetness like a fresh-baked treat or a bouquet of wildflowers, weekend getaways, doing the other's most dreaded chore, stopping everything to hug), but one of the most overlooked and yet most powerful ways to align our hearts before the Lord is to pray together and for each other. The latter is an individual practice, of course, but the former can and will also look different for every couple. I love Jesus's promise that "for where two or three are gathered in my name, there am I among them" (Matthew 18:20). That includes married couples!

For Shaun and me, praying together looks like lying in bed at night and briefly discussing anything we've yet to talk about for the day. Then he'll say the thing he always does: "Praise or pray?" And I will almost always answer, "Praise." And then we'll do what we have done most nights for almost twenty years of marriage—spend the last several minutes before we fall asleep asking the God who made us one flesh to hear our prayers and then thanking Him for His good gifts (including each other). It's such a simple practice but one that I cherish and very much hope we will still be doing at eighty-five, should the Lord grant us so many years.

In It for the Long Haul

Prioritizing marriage when there are children underfoot (or even towering over you as my teenage boys do)—needing, asking, wanting—is *hard*. And yet the rewards are evident in a relationship with your spouse that grows with your family, instead of diminishing with each new parenting struggle. As sad as the thought sometimes makes me, my children will not always live under the same roof with Shaun and me. They will fly the nest, and my relationship with them will morph and shift. Many aspects of my importance in their lives will diminish. And one very strange, very distant-seeming day, it will just be Shaun and me again.

I don't want to wake up one day, when my kids are married with children of their own, and realize I no longer recognize the man next to me in bed. Not only that, but I want to model for my children that they cannot (should not!) take the place of the one human to whom I pledged my lifelong love, loyalty, and passion. Doing so would be a great disservice to my own marriage and to their future spouses.

If it feels like nothing will ever be the same in your marriage once you have kids, you're right. And that can be such a good thing. Children ensure that, if we want our wedding vows to deepen and become richer by the year, we will have to fight for intimacy, joy, and shared vision. Children can keep us from complacency. And ultimately, children help sharpen our focus and unify our purpose, and if we're willing to push past the hard to press on toward the good, they can be one of the best things that ever happened to our marriage.

Abbie is a very capable and talented woman. In many of the areas of home-management she mentioned, it would be laughable for me to grab the rudder and expect to steer as well. But this doesn't mean that I don't help paddle from time to time. While I trust her to perform those tasks unaided, our relationship benefits from sharing in them, even when it isn't necessary.

When I pitch in to help (very slowly and methodically) chop vegetables while Abbie cooks, or she hands me tools while I repair a sink, we are establishing a practice of doing life together rather than separately.

We shouldn't forget to have fun together too! Though we may not always share the same interests, we help cement a bond of shared joy when we seek out activities we both enjoy and make the effort to adopt a few of each other's favorite things too. If you don't know what those activities are, try new things together! Sign up for dancing lessons, learn to draw, take up an instrument, go fishing or camping, set common workout goals, try your hand at pickleball, read the same books, build something together, play board games, *lose* at Nertz (if your experience is anything like mine).

Just don't do nothing.

All too often, we can fall into a rhythm of daily life without truly connecting. It's a form of passivity that leaves us vulnerable to getting so caught up in a goal or work, or another relationship (even our kids), that we allow it to draw our affections away from our spouse. We may ultimately find ourselves escaping—pursuing that interest to the point that we resent our spouse for "keeping us" from it.

Being intentional to pursue shared interests fosters an attitude of "getting to" spend time with the one you love.

So I encourage you to be intentional, pay attention, and guard against escapism. Make a reminder to consistently pray over your spouse, seeking God's guidance for ways to meet their current needs, help with their current tasks, or share in their current interests. Even when life is so busy that the thought of something more—even something fun—sounds like hard work, staying connected with your spouse is worth the effort and sets an example of love and togetherness for your children.

 **The Narrative**

THE WORLD'S RESPONSE TO HARD	A CHRISTIAN RESPONSE TO HARD
Believes kids make marriage worse	Knows that children can enhance our marriages as we prioritize the right things
Makes sure that labor is split fifty-fifty	Looks for ways to serve and lighten a spouse's load
Takes a "victimhood" approach to parenting in marriage	Takes responsibility for finding solutions to the ways kids make marriage more challenging

 **Action Steps**

- Commit to speaking (especially) well of (and to!) your spouse for one whole week. Recruit your accountability partner to keep you on track (and do the same for her).
- Plan a "time of focused togetherness" (a "date") within the next several weeks.
- Make a list of areas in which you'd like to grow in your marriage with kids in the house. Then use your date time with your spouse to brainstorm some solutions or tweaks that would make those areas better.

Questions

What are the hardest parts of prioritizing marriage while also being godly parents?

What are some ways that kids make marriage better?

What are some things the world says about marriage and children that directly contradict what the Bible says?

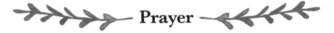

Prayer

Lord, You created marriage in response to the only thing in creation You called "not good": Adam's being alone (Genesis 2:18). You ordained marriage before children, and You have given it to us as a gift but also as a picture of what the relationship between Christ and His church should look like. Help us prioritize our marriages rightly, even when doing so feels like too much effort in a hard season of parenting.

12

The Newborn Stage Is Hard

DYING TO SELF NEVER LOOKED SO CUTE

I t may seem strange to follow up a chapter about the ways in which having kids can enrich our marriages with one about how hard the newborn stage is, but I never want to paint a rosy picture of ease that glosses over (or refuses to recognize) the very real struggles that accompany the daily act of dying to ourselves that is motherhood. Doing so would belie the very point of writing a book called *Hard Is Not the Same Thing as Bad*.

Acknowledge the Hard and Look for the Good

There will be some people—especially those who think they're too deep in a "hard hole" to ever climb out and feel as if I'm "picking on them"—who claim I am

173

peddling a fantasy, burying the hard beneath a pile of feel-good truisms or a peppy can-do spirit. If you've been paying attention at all during the previous eleven chapters, though, you already know that fluff is not really my jam. I'm only interested in real, practical, biblical solutions and growth.

My goal is to acknowledge the legitimacy of hard things in motherhood—without placing them on the pedestal of either insurmountability or worthlessness—so that we can grow in Christlikeness and sharpen our motherhood skills rather than stay stuck in the struggle. After all, "we are his workmanship, created in Christ Jesus for good works, which God prepared beforehand, that we should walk in them" (Ephesians 2:10). The same God who inspired Paul to write, "Rejoice in the Lord always" also prepared for us the good works of mothering that we find ourselves grumbling about under our breath. If that stung a bit to read, know that I felt the same pinch as I typed it.

We can absolutely agree that adopting or pushing a baby out of (or having one cut from) our bodies is hard without relegating it to the "not worth doing" category. We can for sure acknowledge that breastfeeding can be excruciating and complicated without trampling it into the mud of "the worst thing ever." We can hug it out over the brutal reality that is waking up all night to feed a baby and then doing life on four hours of fragmented sleep, without needing to scorn every other aspect of newborn life.

A hot-button label I've seen slapped on a number of things and people recently (including me!) is the term "toxic positivity." Anytime I see a trend like this emerge, I strive to first understand the basis for it and the motivation behind it, and then I compare it to the truth of Scripture. The times I've had the words "toxic positivity" tossed at me have mainly been in response to my encouraging mothers to take their overwhelm to the Lord, instead of venting in front of their children or about them to other mothers. The pushback is sometimes downright hostile and always defensive: "Don't tell me not to complain when I don't like something. I'll complain if I feel like it, thanks very much. If a situation is hard, and I suppress my feelings, I'll eventually blow up. That's toxic positivity."

A Biblical Approach to Venting

From a biblical perspective, this is completely upside down and backwards, at least in part because suppression of feelings is nowhere to be found in Scripture. I'm not telling anyone not to *feel* or that what they're feeling doesn't seem like the "realest" thing in the world *in that moment*. Neither is the Bible. Ever read the Psalms? Job? Lamentations? Any of the minor prophets? These dudes weren't exactly "stuffing" their feelings. Instead, there are literally dozens of examples of "crying out to God" in the Bible. The Israelites petition God for mercy while enslaved to Pharoah (Exodus 2:23). Likewise, Moses begs for help after God frees his people from the Egyptians, and the Israelites then focus their ire on Moses when they get tired and thirsty in the desert (Exodus 17:4). God's chosen people cry out to Him over and over about enemy oppression throughout Judges (3:9; 4:3; 6:7). Nehemiah calls out to God for help when the Jews are surrounded by aggressive forces seeking to stop them from rebuilding the walls of Jerusalem (4:4). David, the poet king, practically makes a career out of airing his frustrations and sorrows to God, noting in Psalm 34:6 that "this poor man cried, and the Lord heard him and saved him out of all his troubles." And even Jesus cries out to His Father as He endures the agony of the cross and the crushing burden of humankind's sin (Matthew 27:46).

The kind of grumbling that vilifies our children and paints motherhood with broad strokes of martyrdom produces havoc, not healing, for our emotional and physical well-being.

Clearly, the Bible sets a precedent for casting our cares on the Lord because He cares for us (1 Peter 5:7), rather than burying them deep in our souls until they erupt with suppressed rage when we least expect. But grumbling that vilifies our children and paints motherhood with broad strokes of martyrdom produces havoc, not healing, for our emotional and physical well-being.

Envy Is a Joy Killer

Proverbs 14:30 says, "A tranquil heart gives life to the flesh, but envy makes the bones rot." If you're wondering what envy has to do with complaining about our kids, let me just say this: So much of our discontentment with our circumstances arises from comparing our own lot in life to someone else's (either because they don't have kids yet or their kids seem to be easier than ours). Or we envy our own previous habits of sleeping in, eating a meal without interruptions, or spontaneously going to a movie at midnight. We scorn the growth and beauty that come from caring for a new little life, all for the sake of an idealized version of our former selves.

And how do I know this? Because of my own struggles at times to adjust to the role of new mama. And because of the frequent messages I receive, saying things like "I've wanted to be a mother my whole life. And it didn't come easily. We tried for years. But now that it's here, I find myself running from the struggles because I had no idea how much selfishness I would have to confront when I finally got the one thing in the world I yearned for most."

I am convinced down to the very roots of my soul that no apparent mothering sacrifice is too great when compared with the joy of truly possessing a "tranquil heart," not to mention the health benefits it brings (bitterness is truly toxic, yo). But neither will I deny that it can take time (years!) and the transforming work of the Holy Spirit in our hearts to reach that place of being at peace with the hard. And not just at peace with the newborn stage. But we'll talk about that more in a minute.

Toxic Positivity or a Lack of Empathy?

Of course, just because an encouragement to lean into the struggles of motherhood without complaining *isn't* toxic doesn't mean that we won't encounter genuinely off-putting responses to our pain. When one reader used the term "toxic positivity" to refer to the way some moms interact with each other, I asked her what she meant, expecting something similar to what I've already described.

Instead, she relayed the following conversation:

Them: "How's it going with the new little guy?"

Mama: "It's going well. He's such a sweetheart. I mean, we aren't sleeping much, and feeding is really painful, but we're adjusting and really enjoying our time together."

Them: "There are so many people who would give anything to be sleep deprived because of a baby. You should really count your blessings!"

Mama: [*Exits stage left with smoke issuing from ears.*]

If you, too, feel at a complete loss to respond with equanimity to those who refuse to "weep with those who weep"—but seriously! We're not even weeping! Just acknowledging facts!—may I suggest that, as my friend Jennifer puts it, "These people aren't being toxically positive so much as lacking basic empathy."

And if any stage requires maximum empathy, it's the newborn stage (although it's neck and neck with toddlerdom). *Especially* for first-time moms. In a culture that often mocks the idea of proactively educating ourselves on how to care for children ("This isn't the 1950s!"), we have an epidemic of first-time mamas with zero experience in basic baby care (diapers! bath time! simple sickness remedies! feeding! routines! laundry!), and it shows in the panicked messages I receive daily.

"I never learned how to…"

"I have no idea what I'm doing."

"She won't stop crying!"

"I'm at a complete loss."

"No one ever modeled this for me."

I would argue that motherly instinct is real but also inherited and bolstered by the examples of women who have gone before us. Certainly, our intuition can be muffled by conflicting opinions online and too little sleep, by too much sensory overload and too little wisdom from seasoned mothers. Add in recovering from delivery (which is a bit like recovering from running a marathon after squatting at the finish line over a case of exploding dynamite), waddling around in adult diapers, sporting constantly milk-stained three-day-old sweats, and trying to figure out why one breast is perpetually and painfully larger than the other, and you have the kind of hard that is equal parts comical and tragical.

I would argue that motherly instinct is real but also inherited and bolstered by the examples of women who have gone before us.

Clueless but in Love

When a precious little seven-pound, five-ounce miracle named Ezra made me a mama, I remember marveling at the fuzz on his shoulders (I learned it was called "lanugo") and the way his perfectly formed fingers sported tiny half-moons at their cuticles. His labor was long (forty-four hours), his delivery short (two quick pushes), and my recovery (relatively) easy. I was twenty-three years old, active and healthy, lacking in nothing physical and everything experiential.

I will probably never regain your sympathy for anything else I tell you after I admit this, but here goes: Ezra started sleeping eight hours a night consistently at a week old. I know. Easiest newborn ever. And he nursed like a champ, gaining weight as readily as a pregnant woman who so much as looks at a cookie.

But you know what? I still had so much anxiety about bedtime with him. Would he Houdini his way out of the swaddle? Had I burped him enough? Had I burped him too much? Was that a thing? Why, if I had burped him just the right amount, did he keep squirming and bunching his little body up like that?

I distinctly remember lying in bed at night, stiff as a poker, as Shaun snored gently beside me, and feeling completely (and bleakly) alone. I remember thinking, "This is it. This is my life forever. I will always be lying here in the dark, listening to my newborn's strange little grunts and squeaks, terrified they will turn into wails, and I'll have no idea how to soothe him. Unless it's another forty-five-minute nursing session. And I'm the only one who can do that. So, yeah. This is it. Goodbye, normalcy. Hello, constant low-level panic."

I had no idea that Ezra was using me as a human pacifier (until my second, who sucked down his meals in a mere five minutes on each side, proved it to me). I had no idea what "baby blues" were or that nighttime is always the hardest. I had no idea I'd feel less alone after multiple consecutive hours of sleep and then a little bit of time outside in the sunshine. I had no idea that when you refuse to give a baby who constantly wants to nurse an actual pacifier because you'll never be "that mom," he might find his own fingers by three weeks. And fingers are way harder to "take away" than pacifiers. I had no idea that I could simultaneously love a tiny human so much and find him somewhat terrifying.

 I had no idea that I could simultaneously love a tiny human so much and find him somewhat terrifying.

I had no idea.

Maybe you can relate?

Friends, I know how hard it is to find, much to your chagrin, that much of your body's landscape has suddenly become foreign and misshapen beneath your fingertips. The soft doughiness of a once-firm midsection. The bluish veins snaking haphazardly through engorged breasts. The balding temples slowly recovered by baby hairs that grow in like a Civil War general's sideburns.

When you're a complete novice at being in charge of fulfilling 99 percent of a small human's desires and needs, even if he *is* a newborn as completely normal (though abnormally great at sleeping) as Ezra was, the learning curve is steep, and the self-doubt is strong. I can only imagine the added stress of a sweet baby with disabilities or a mama who has multiples as her first babies.

And yet, by God's grace, we muddle through, and many of us even do it again!

Nothing Lasts Forever

Want to hear something crazy? Despite the fact that I have been on the brand-new-baby roller coaster eight times (doubling up on the fun twice with twins) and know full well what a challenge it is, I now *adore* the newborn stage like few other things in life.

The grunts that once shot pangs of anxiety along my nerves? *They're adorable.*

The burps that stressed me so much? *Eh, we get what we can. The rest work themselves out.*

The pacifier I swore I'd never use? *Here, baby doll. Let's get you some comfort. Didn't like that brand? I'll find you another one.*

The middle-of-the-night wakeups? *Still not my favorite, but sometimes I just stare at their small, perfectly composed features while they nurse, and I thank God for my ability to be their safe place and source of life-giving sustenance.*

Oh, and the pure bliss of lying on the couch "trapped" beneath the weight of a sweet-smelling newborn? *Cannot get enough.*

In fact, even though my second set of twins slept the least well of any of my babies through their first year, even though they were the fussiest, even though it hurt the most to feed them due to gnarly tongue-ties that went undiagnosed for nine weeks (despite my pursuing a diagnosis), I was less stressed by the hard than I had ever been.

Why? Because by the time they were born, I had fourteen years of proof that, far from lasting forever—as my overwhelmed brain imagined when I only had Ezra—the newborn phase is the only period of life where time actually speeds up. Pure scientific facts, folks. Ask any mama who's done it a few times, and she'll back me up.

And since I now know how fleeting those days of milky breath and petal-soft skin truly are, I can choose to see them as a thing to be treasured rather than a chore to be dreaded. I know not everyone loves the newborn phase, even after doing it a few times, but I would be surprised if they denied that each subsequent time feels less like trying to blaze the Oregon Trail with a pocketknife. This is true even if you "only" have two kids. It's incredible how our brains and bodies adapt and expand with knowledge and experience.

We Do Get Better, by God's Grace

Caring so constantly for another human being exercises different muscles (literally and figuratively) than anything else we encounter in life. Those muscles get sore. Excruciatingly so, at times. But then, they get stronger and more effective. The newborn phase has the potential to grow not only our practical skills (pretty sure I can change a poopy diaper in fifteen seconds flat) but our resilience, our gratitude, and, most importantly, our dependence on Jesus.

Caring so constantly for another human being exercises different muscles (literally and figuratively) than anything else we encounter in life.

Isaiah 26:3 says, "You keep him in perfect peace whose mind is stayed on you, because he trusts in you." Isaiah must have been a man who never dealt with a baby who wouldn't stop crying, right? And yet there have been moments (not every one of them, mind you) when, as I bounced and shushed and swayed the twinbies while they both howled in misery, I prayed Jesus's name over and over in my mind and was enveloped by a supernatural calm that had nothing to do with the chaos of my circumstances.

As we "put off the old self with its practices" (like self-pity, complaining, blame shifting, and laziness) and "put on the new self, which is being renewed in knowledge after the image of its creator," we discover just how true it is that "Christ is all, and in all" (Colossians 3:9-11).

I have noticed a phenomenon that used to puzzle me: Young moms would message me and say, "It's cool that you can teach fitness classes, but I can't do that because I have a two-year-old and a newborn in the house." Or "I'm not in a season of meal planning because I've got a new baby." Or "Mine are only eighteen months apart, so I can't get much done during the day." What confused me was that I was receiving these messages while nursing two newborns who were seven *minutes* apart while their nineteen-month-old brother bounced on the bed near my elbow.

The logic seems to be "You have ten kids, so your capacity must be greater than mine as a new mom of two, and your hard can't feel as real."

Wait, what?

It was Shaun who pointed out that, although this reasoning seems faulty at first glance, it's actually reflective of a core truth of motherhood. As counterintuitive as it seems to tell someone who had five little boys under six at the time (and five more older children to parent) about the especially hard time you're having with your two under three, the *assumption* behind such a message makes sense: "This is easier for you because you've had more practice and experience."

The good news is there's some truth to this. Is it hard to have five little boys under six, including two infants, regardless of how long you've been a mother? Absolutely! But do they *feel* less intimidating than two under two did back when I was a brand-new mama? You bet your stretch marks they do!

And that should be an encouragement to anyone who finds herself still slogging through the "will this ever get easier" stage. Because it does! The Lord is faithful to stretch our capabilities with every trial we face so that, even if we encounter much harder situations than we did when we were sure we would never be okay again, we no longer buckle beneath the weight of inexperience. As God gives us new opportunities for relying on His strength, we can say with Paul, "Not that I have already obtained this or am already perfect, but I press on to make it my own, because Christ Jesus has made me his own" (Philippians 3:12).

The Gold Standard of Comfort

Paul is specifically referring to sharing in the sufferings of Christ and becoming like Him in attaining "the resurrection from the dead" (verses 9-11), but I would argue that the willing, self-sacrificial love of a mama for her newborn serves as a very real example of sharing in Christ's sufferings.

On top of that, Paul establishes mamas as the gold standard for tender care

Not that I have already obtained
this or am already perfect, but I
press on to make it my own, because
Christ Jesus has made me his own.
PHILIPPIANS 3:12

when he says, "We were gentle among you, like a nursing mother taking care of her own children" (1 Thessalonians 2:7). Sidenote: If you're a mama who doesn't fit into a "box" I've talked about yet in this chapter but have cared for your newborn, then this is you. Adoptive mamas, birth mamas, bottle-feeding mamas, nursing mamas, C-section mamas, no-med mamas, "crunchy" mamas, and "traditional" mamas *all* understand that the newborn stage is one of the most precious and most trying times of any woman's life.

Our conscious choice to pour love into tiny image-bearers who have been entrusted to us by their Creator—even when it's harder than we imagined possible—is one very practical way that we can model self-denial, taking up our cross daily, and following Jesus (Matthew 16:24). After all, "those who belong to Christ Jesus have crucified the flesh with its passions and desires. If we live by the Spirit, let us also keep in step with the Spirit" (Galatians 5:24-25).

Our conscious choice to pour love into tiny image-bearers who have been entrusted to us by their Creator—even when it's harder than we imagined possible—is one very practical way that we can model self-denial, taking up our cross daily, and following Jesus.

Praise God we have His Spirit who gives us the ability to walk the challenging road of mothering a newborn with the kind of steadfast commitment that feels impossible in our very human flesh. And as we do so, we declare to a perplexed world that, far from being toxic, choosing joy—even in the hard stages of motherhood—is life-giving, freeing, and worth the effort.

DAD THOUGHT

I really don't want to write down my "Dad Thought" on newborns. And it's not because I don't like babies. I love them. There's just something about their helpless trust (snuggles!), their lack of self-consciousness (baby noises!), their wonder at experiencing each new part of the world around them (wide eyes!), and the incredibly cute, wrap-you-around-their-wrinkled-little-finger package they come in that I just can't get enough of. Case in point: If my babies fall asleep on my chest on the couch, I'd better be in a good position, because I will do nothing to jeopardize the joy of being "trapped" beneath their sleeping weight until that nap is done.

So why don't I want to write down my thought?

Because I don't know whether the Lord has more babies in store for us, and if I write down the conviction He's given me, then I will most certainly be expected to follow through on its conclusion should He bless us with another baby (or two).

And yet, "Those who say that they belong to the Lord must turn away from wrongdoing" (2 Timothy 2:19 GNT).

And the first step toward turning away from sin is confession, so here goes:

I'm not *entitled* to more sleep than my wife.

Nor am I due less-interrupted sleep than my wife. And yet, despite knowing what a physical drain it is on her, I still do the minimum at night I can get away with because getting up in the middle of the night is hard, and I just don't want to do it.

And all the dads said, "Is that really so bad?"

And all the mamas said, "That'll preach!"

It isn't that I haven't improved over the years. I have. With each kid, I do a little more, and I can distinctly remember (because how could you forget?) waking up every forty-five minutes all night long for days on end with the twinbies who were, to put it mildly, not our best sleepers.

But you know what? As soon as our babies start to improve and the absolute minimum requirement lowers, I'm right there with it, practically calculating how many times I can get away with not getting up before it becomes a "problem."

Sure, there may be some truth to the fact that moms are wired to wake at the sound of a baby crying while dads slumber on (I regularly wake up in the morning having never heard the baby cry or the toddler come in). But I do wonder how much of that is simply because we dads tell ourselves we don't want or need to get up while our wives tell themselves they must. The power of suggestion over whether that cry pierces my veil of sleep is probably stronger than I think.

I don't believe midnight awakenings have to be even steven. Depending on night-feeding choices, dads might not even have the equipment unless Mom pumps. Yet even if she does it all, simply waking to hold her hand and talk quietly from time to time can do so much to show her she's not alone, especially when we know she's experiencing postpartum struggles.

(Abbie inserted approximately ten exclamation points when she read that last sentence, so I think I'm onto something.)

Dads, we need to view the newborn stage with a heart of service, not a calculation of minimum requirements, and that includes nighttime. We must pay attention to the needs of our wives and genuinely share in this hard task after we've *both* so often had a long day.

Mamas, if you find yourselves drowning, instead of resenting the fact that your husband doesn't intuitively step up his newborn game, speak up! Kindly explain the areas of greatest stress in this season and ask him to help out in specific ways. Chances are, he'll appreciate (and respond to) a direct request when the alternative is a cold shoulder or a frustrated wife.

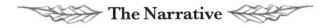

The Narrative

THE WORLD'S RESPONSE TO HARD	A CHRISTIAN RESPONSE TO HARD
Views encouragement to look for the good in the newborn stage as "toxic positivity"	Knows that the Bible calls us to "rejoice in all things"
Resents the loss of bodily autonomy and free time	Realizes that a newborn's total dependency is a fleeting gift
Mothers from a place of constant overwhelm	Views the overwhelm as an opportunity to cast *all* our cares on the Lord

Action Steps

- Memorize and meditate on Ephesians 2:10: "We are his workmanship, created in Christ Jesus for good works, which God prepared beforehand, that we should walk in them."

- If you're out of your first round of the newborn stage, write a letter (or at least a list) to your younger self of things you wish you'd known before becoming the mom of a tiny infant. If you're still in the newborn stage or about to be in it, ask God to send a godly woman who could share her list with you.

- Sign up to take a meal to a new mom if you can. Or offer to clean her bathrooms or fold her laundry. Nothing makes a new mom feel less alone than knowing someone else has been in her shoes and "made it."

Questions

What are the best parts about the newborn stage? What are the hardest? How do both push us toward the Lord?

What are some ways that our newborns' reliance on us should mirror our trust in the Lord?

How is "toxic positivity" very different from godly rejoicing (even in hard things)?

Prayer

Jesus, thank You for coming as a helpless infant to save us, but also, in part, to underscore what a blessing little innocent newborns are to the world. Their utter dependence is trying at times but also precious in its trust and unconditional love. Help us to see them for the treasure they are and to understand just how fleeting our time with them truly is.

13

Toddlers Are Hard

CHOOSING TO BE THE ADULT WHEN WE WANT TO THROW TANTRUMS TOO

Some of my favorite people in the world are three-year-olds. I have two of them right now, and they are the snuggliest, happiest, most endearing little creatures on the planet. It's the best!

But do you know who some of the most frustrating people in the world are? Also three-year-olds. I have two of them right now, and they are the most exhausting, most maddening, least emotionally regulated little creatures on the planet. It's the hardest! (Notice I did not say "the worst.")

The "Awesome Hardness" of Toddlers

I can't fully grasp how it's possible to be the best and the hardest at the same time, and neither can a three-year-old.

189

Or a two-year-old. Or an eighteen-month-old. Toddlers have no idea why they're so amazing and so crazy-making all at once, and even if they did have a clue, they wouldn't be able to tell us, because their communication skills are pretty much limited to "NO," "MINE," "juice," "up," and "potty" (if we've successfully run the dreaded potty-training gauntlet, that is).

Yes, I know this is a broad statement. Our seventh child, Honor, would say things like, "Actually, Mother, I would like the blue one" when he was twenty months old. The child could have delivered a State of the Union address at four.

In general, though, one of the most significant contributors to the delicate tension of the "awesome hardness" most toddlers inhabit is their struggle to gain more independence without either the words to express exactly what they want or the frontal lobe development to want something reasonable to begin with.

Toddlers…struggle to gain more independence without either the words to express exactly what they want or the frontal lobe development to want something reasonable to begin with.

They're desperate for a sip of scorching black coffee because if Mama loves it, then it *must* be scrumptious. Our insistence, "Coffee is yucky and hot. *Hurt you. No touch,*" only sweetens their anticipation for that moment when we turn our backs, and they can finally sneak a taste of Mama's yummy "morning juice."

And what happens when they finally achieve their cherished goal? Weeping. Wailing. Gagging. Spitting. Gnashing of teeth. Oh, and the Gaze of Utter Betrayal. How *could* we exploit their innocence and lure them into an opportunity to poison and scald themselves like that? What kind of mothers *are* we? (I write this from a place of utter abhorrence for coffee, but I know I'm in the minority, and you could substitute just about any hot food or liquid into this scenario with—literally—painful accuracy).

I get more emails, DMs, comments, and internet rants regarding toddlers than any other topic I talk about. I'd probably receive smoke signals about them if mamas could figure out how to send a message using the aftermath of the burnt toast catastrophe that happened while they were distracted cleaning up another pee puddle.

The Path of Most Resistance

I hear you, friends. I do. I didn't start this book with a description of Nola's car-seat woes leading to a "hard is not the same thing as bad" revelation because I've never dealt with the kind of constant drip (or flood, depending on the day) of whining, demands, and tantrums that leave you doubting your capacity to "keep it together" on a daily basis.

In fact, I feel duty bound to report to you that, of the ten toddlers I have parented so far, *two* are what I would have called truly "easy," with a possible third thrown in for good measure as a "total stinker but such a fun personality he didn't bother me a bit." The rest have at some point, and in a variety of ways, tested every limit to my endurance, every trick in my parenting bag, and every misguided belief in my own sufficiency.

No childhood stage has forced me to take a harder, more clear-eyed look at my own natural and ungodly tendencies toward laziness, impatience, and self-ishness than toddlerdom. No age has humbled me more deeply than three years old. No behavior has driven me battier than the "I want it! WHY ARE YOU GIVING ME THAT THING I ASKED FOR?" seesaw logic that is a two-year-old's everyday mode of communication. And no developmental roadblock has made me more grateful that I am capable of boldly approaching the throne of God's grace (Hebrews 4:16) than a very small child's inability to express herself in anything more than piteous wails of "Mama!"

That last bit—our ability to talk to *our* Father every moment of every day, without fear of ever wearing out our welcome—is the one that should sober us up a bit when we find ourselves making a mad dash for our emergency stash of chocolate (only to realize it's running low just two days after we bought it) as soon as we get our toddler down for a nap. Chocolate is delicious, and eating a treat during naptime can be a fantastic way to recharge. But it's a poor substitute for the chance to "delight yourself in the LORD" and discover that "he will give you the desires of your heart. Commit your way to the LORD; trust in him, and he will act" (Psalm 37:4-5).

Maybe you're thinking, "But chocolate and alone time *were* the desires of my heart, and the two-year-old is boycotting his nap like his life depends on it. C'mon, Lord!" Let me ask you this: Do you also want to be a more patient person? A more empathetic one? Gentler? Kinder? Are these some of the "desires of your heart" too? What if the very avenue for maturity that we long to walk down is the path of *most* resistance that looks a whole lot like our very cute, very challenging toddler? What if the Lord *is* acting for our best benefit and His greatest glory by allowing us to encounter yet another "I do it myself" mess on the pantry floor, another pair of pooped-in underwear from the "potty-trained" three-year-old, another emotional disintegration over his favorite shirt being in the wash?

*What if the very avenue for maturity that we long to walk down is the path of **most** resistance that looks a whole lot like our very cute, very challenging toddler?*

What if our subconscious (or even blatantly stated) desire for an "easy kid" is stunting our spiritual growth?

If your answer is "So be it. I'll stay where I am spiritually if it means I get a break from the nonsense," you're not alone. Sometimes, when we're maxed out on emotional bandwidth, "spiritual growth" sounds like a euphemism for "bring on the hard," and we're just not up for it.

I will boast all the more gladly of my weaknesses, so that the power of Christ may rest upon me.

2 CORINTHIANS 12:9

Boasting in Our Weakness

I have good news for you, friends: This is *all of us* in our own strength. Wait, sorry. That's not the good news yet. The good news is that our not being up for another epic "eat your dinner" tussle is no indication that our heavenly Father feels similarly burned out. Nor is He surprised by our needing His help. On the contrary, we can declare with Paul that God's grace is sufficient, for His power "is made perfect in weakness." This verse rings especially true because, in the verses immediately preceding it, Paul admits to begging God for an easier way, and the Almighty's response is not "Consider it done," but essentially, "I AM ENOUGH." Paul's conclusion is inspiring: "Therefore I will boast all the more gladly of my weaknesses, so that the power of Christ may rest upon me...For when I am weak, then I am strong" (2 Corinthians 12:9-10).

Declaring strength in our greatest moments of weakness makes no logical sense, but we've already talked plenty about how God's thoughts are not our thoughts, nor His ways our ways. "For as the heavens are higher than the earth, so are my ways higher than your ways and my thoughts than your thoughts" (Isaiah 55:8-9). We can see this so clearly in how He has wired small humans to both test our sanity and fill our hearts with a fiercely protective love that says, "He may be a little wrecking ball, but he's *my* little wrecking ball!"

If toddlers were all spitfire defiance and demands to drink out of the sippy cup in the way that *always* ends in a face full of water and screaming, we would (and sometimes do) despise the rich opportunities for growth inherent in peacefully weathering the torrential emotional downpours that have the potential to reap "a harvest of righteousness" (James 3:18). By contrast, if they were all angelic sweetness, we might never realize that we need to grow in the first place.

Few of us will find ourselves in the latter condition, though, so when we do realize our lack, the question quickly becomes "What now?"

What can we do on a practical level to parlay the Holy Spirit–inspired efforts we make to exercise "patience, gentleness, and self-control" into the kind of growth and skill that allows us to guide our sweet and saucy toddlers toward Jesus? Oh, and sanity. Not to mention the honor and obedience to parents that

Ephesians 6:1-3 describes as "the first commandment with a promise, that it may go well with you and that you may live long in the land."

So glad you asked, because I've got a few thoughts:

We must own our adulthood.

If the number of T-shirts declaring the wearer's inability to "adult today" is any indication, we live in a society that glorifies a "Peter Pan" approach to life. "Growing up is boring! If I'm not feeling up to my responsibilities, I just won't do them!" I wish I were exaggerating, but as rental property owners, Shaun and I have encountered more tenants than we'd like to admit who were certainly old enough to qualify as adults but not emotionally or morally mature enough to act like one. Inevitably, with these types, we were left with unpaid rent, trashed properties, and even, in one case, a literal fire to put out on Christmas Day.

How much more negatively impactful is it to our children when we fail to "adult" in our interactions with them?

I get messages regularly from moms who describe their toddlers' antics and conclude, "She's driving me crazy! How am I supposed to deal with this without losing my mind?"

To which I almost always reply with a gentle reminder that there is only one adult in the scenario that they're describing—and it's the mama messaging me. On top of that, the verse that follows the one above—that children should obey their parents—says, "Fathers, do not provoke your children to anger, but bring them up in the discipline and instruction of the Lord" (Ephesians 6:4). I know we're not fathers, but I have a strong suspicion mothers don't get a free pass to throw fits or exasperate our children either.

I follow up my "We're the adults here!" pep talk with practical advice relevant to the situation whenever possible, but sometimes all a toddler mom needs to snap out of victim mode is the reminder that tantrums are for tiny people, not adults. We *know* better (or, at least, we should) because we've had more experience and more practice at life. Our active choice to step into the maturity and authority the Lord has entrusted to us as adults goes a long way toward defusing frustrating situations charged with hectic feelings and unreasonable reactions that often stem from something as simple as a missed nap or snack.

*Sometimes all a toddler mom needs to snap out of victim mode is the reminder that tantrums are for tiny people, not adults. We **know** better (or, at least, we should) because we've had more experience and more practice at life.*

A deplorable trend floating around the internet a few years ago featured young moms serving their toddlers trays full of carefully curated foods, some of which were carved into messages like "You piss me off," or even "F*** you." I remember experiencing an icy-hot wave of shock and visceral anger the first time I saw one of these videos, complete with a precious little girl giggling and clapping in oblivious delight that her mother was serving her "MY LETTERS!"

Of course, this mom was pulling such a stunt for the likes and comments (which consisted primarily of gems such as "This is me as a mom. Toddlers are the worst!"). But there are ways—including telling stories in a mocking manner that exploits our children's struggles—in which we can participate in similarly heartbreaking and damaging episodes of "toddler hate" if we do not firmly and steadfastly hold to the simple truth: "I'm the adult. Not only that, but I'm also the mama. I have been given the ability by God to choose the good in His strength, no matter how much easier it would be to dwell on the hard."

We must recognize the truth of developmental limitations.

Similar to the need to acknowledge ourselves as the adult in the situation, it's so important to recognize the very real limitations our toddlers have in their abilities to: communicate, emotionally self-regulate, use linear reasoning, and put anyone else first.

So much of what *feels* personally insulting isn't personal at all but an impulse arising from a brain that simply lacks the tools needed to exercise self-control and awareness of others. Far from using these facts as excuses to let unkind or complaining behavior slide, our knowledge of where our small children are developmentally can better inform the kinds of training, praying, teaching, practice, and support we can use to help them grow in maturity.

Very young children have the capacity to learn "please," "thank you," and "excuse me" if we model these phrases for them and consistently remind them of the appropriate scenarios in which to use them. I have encountered some moms online who discourage teaching toddlers any of these things, arguing that they're too young to fully understand their meaning. I disagree! In fact, it is *because* my toddlers have no concept of gratitude or politeness that I begin this training early and practice it with consistency. That way, when they're old enough to grasp the concept, all the practice we've done will be married with comprehension, which is a beautiful union.

This can also hold true for teaching our children to eat the foods we make them for dinner. "Thankful bites" (where at least a small taste is attempted out of gratitude to the one who prepared the food) are a great way to encourage our children to at least try everything on their plates when they're very young (and also to teach them to express thankfulness, whether they *feel* thankful or not).

Each child's ability to fully grasp the importance of a varied diet (um, hello, I'm an adult, and I still wish I could just skip some good-for-me foods) will vary by age and temperament. We *could* allow our small children a wandering, free-range grazing approach that wreaks havoc on our family's ability to sit down together at dinner (or eat out at a restaurant) and enjoy each other (a concept that may feel laughable in a season of only littles but can be achieved with repetitive effort and consistency). However, we gain more peace in the long run by creating a dinner framework that acknowledges developmental limitations but doesn't use them as excuses not to try.

Practically speaking, this means we often end up with tiny children in our laps as we help them eat. Could we require that they stay in their chairs, perfectly still and neat? I suppose we could *insist* on such a thing, but I've found that requiring perfect "seat attendance" from younger toddlers who are still learning the "rules of dinner" usually results in an ugly battle of wills and in tears (for the mom and the child).

Practice the good stuff!

I have my hills to die on, certainly, but requiring things that children aren't developmentally ready to achieve is not one of them. (In case you're wondering, my three-year-olds sit in their seats 90 percent of the time after lots of practice, while their four-year-old brother stays in his—hypothetically—100 percent of the time). The important thing is that, even if they're not ready to master them yet, we introduce new concepts and practice because (a) this sometimes reveals a child who *is* ready earlier than other kids his age and (b) while practice does not actually make perfect, it does produce consistency, either for good habits or bad. And so we practice the good stuff!

One more thought on developmental awareness: I know of some moms who are so concerned with brain development, the latest neuroscientific revelation, and childhood phases that they work themselves into a tizzy over "Wonder Weeks" and "cognitive leaps." While it can be helpful to know that many babies go through a sleep regression at four months, it can also produce undue anxiety and even dread as we anticipate a stage that we may never even encounter (for example, only one of my children experienced significant sleep habit changes at four months).

Many years ago, I had an acquaintance who was convinced her toddler was teething almost constantly because she needed a concrete explanation each time he was cranky or had trouble sleeping. Once when we were visiting their home, I overheard her husband wearily mutter, "He's been 'getting molars' every week for three straight years; it's a medical miracle."

It's important to remember that children are just like adults in that they have hard moments, hours, and even days (okay, and weeks and months too). The reason could be anything from teething or another developmental milestone to something they ate, a bad dream, an allergic reaction, or any infinitesimal number of other possibilities we may never even consider.

It's good to pay attention and be a proactive proponent for our children's health and emotional well-being. But obsessing over whether their behavior fits a developmental box produces more stress than peace, which inevitably spills over into our husband's and children's lives as well.

It's good to pay attention and be a proactive proponent for our children's health and emotional well-being. But obsessing over whether their behavior fits a developmental box produces more stress than peace, which inevitably spills over into our husband's and children's lives as well.

We must be willing to acknowledge our children's sin natures.

Yes, it's true that toddlers' brains are less developed than ours, and nine times out of ten, their agitation over tangled shoelaces stems from a desperation to master a task they just don't have the fine motor skills for yet.

But we would be remiss as Christian mamas if we ignored the biblical fact that "through one man sin entered into the world, and death through sin, and so death spread to all mankind, because all sinned" (Romans 5:12 NASB). In this verse, the Greek for both "man" and "mankind" is a form of *anthropos*, which means human beings in general. It does *not* mean a person of a certain age or developmental capacity but rather any member of the human race. The correlative Hebrew word, *adam*, speaks to the very individual that Paul is referring to as the avenue through which sin entered the hearts of all humankind, including our precious baby sleeping so peacefully in his crib.

If *your* heart squeezes at the very suggestion that a sweet toddler, with his winsome, tiny-toothed grin and pudgy, dimpled hands could qualify as something so sordid-sounding as a "sinner," mine too. And yet I cannot ignore Proverbs 22:15, which says, "Folly is bound up in the heart of a child." And for those who will inevitably argue that "folly" simply means "lack of wisdom or experience," the Hebrew word here is *ivveleth*, which has its root in—you guessed it—"evil."

Through Adam, sin (with its evil intentions) entered the world and infected all of us. We can either revolt against the unequivocal biblical truth that from the moment of birth we are, all of us, dead in our sins (Ephesians 2:1) and in desperate need of the redeeming power of Jesus's blood on the cross. Or we can rejoice in the knowledge that, even though "the wages of sin is death...the free gift of God is eternal life in Christ Jesus our Lord" (Romans 6:23). And that goes for our little ones as well! Christ's sacrifice is good news for our toddlers just as much as for their mamas, and we have the joyous opportunity to declare the gospel from the moment they have ears to hear it.

Certainly, our toddlers' meltdowns, even those stemming from a sinful urge to put their desires before anyone else's, carry a different weight of responsibility than our own knowing disobedience of God's laws. But the fact remains that, unchecked, our children's sin will lead to eternal separation from their Maker as they cross the threshold of accountability from sinful ignorance into sinful willfulness.

And so, to anyone who gasps at how "unloving" it is for me to teach my young children the difference between right and wrong with words like "sin" and "God's righteousness," I'd say this: The most *unloving* thing I could possibly do to the child I adore, the child I would willingly die for, is to *not* preach the indisputable reality of sin (the child's, our own, the world's) and the incredible truth of the Savior who already paid the penalty for it.

Just as being aware of developmental limitations can free us from a tendency to feel personally insulted by our small children's disobedience, so also an awareness that they, like us, will struggle with sinful anger, pride, jealousy, covetousness, deceitfulness, and rebellion can prime our compassion pumps with a cognizance of their need to be covered in prayer, God's Word, discipleship, discipline, and the truth of the gospel.

What's more, an awareness that they, *unlike* us, have not experienced years of spiritual growth under the guidance of the Holy Spirit puts in stark relief the responsibility we have as Christian mothers to pray fervently for their salvation—while teaching them the truth of the consequences of sin. When we consider our own relationships with the Lord and our toddlers' lack thereof, it's easier to not "grow weary of doing good," trusting that "in due season, we will reap, if we do not give up" (Galatians 6:9).

This is my all-time favorite motherhood verse that's not actually about motherhood, specifically. And yes, the "reaping" it refers to is one of eternal rewards rather than "good behavior" from our children. But the principle of planting seeds of righteousness that only God can cause to grow in our young children's minds and hearts still applies. Even if "all" we ever gain is becoming more like Christ in the process of disciplining, training, and loving our toddlers as a mirror of the way that God loves, disciplines, and trains all of us, we will have, indeed, reaped a rich harvest.

Toddlers are hard, friends.
And delightful!

Toddlers are hard, friends. And delightful! But sometimes the hard feels like it's winning, and the only option appears to be throwing a tantrum right along with them. Thankfully, we have the Holy Spirit (and other moms who love the Lord) to remind us of the truth that toddler tantrums can be incredible learning opportunities as we pray for our sweet kiddos, lovingly correct them, and teach them valuable tools for managing their disappointment, anger, and overwhelm, *while* modeling tools for gaining victory over our own sinful responses.

Rather than viewing toddlers as a hammer meant to smash our wills to mother with excellence, may we see them as a form of holy sandpaper, which smooths our sharp tongues and softens our harsh reactions, leaving behind a pliable heart poised toward the truth of God's mercy, goodness, and love for every sinner, young and old.

TRIED AND TRUE TODDLER TACTICS

Of all the toddler topics I encounter, the most asked after is discipline. People want to know what consequences they should dole out to their small children, preferably those that will magically quash an undesirable behavior with the least amount of effort on the parents' part. And while I don't typically speak at length about specific discipline methods on social media (largely due to the volatile and erratic nature of the internet on all sides of the "discipline" debate coupled with a God- and husband-prompted commitment to protect my family first), I am happy to share some of the proactive measures we take when our young children are struggling with rage or outbursts.

- *Calm.* Maybe it should go without saying, but I'll say it anyway: Losing our cool will never help our agitated children regain theirs.

- *Breathing practice.* We have had one child, in particular, who struggled with "rage monster" tendencies for several years. One huge help was teaching him to breathe in through his nose and out through his mouth (yep, "labor breathing") to help calm his heart rate, distract him from his anger, and think more clearly. If your child is resistant to this at first (or even periodically after he's become accustomed to it), that's completely normal. It's your job to persevere in modeling and helping him participate in calm breathing (remain firm but very calm in your insistence that he at least practice a few breaths). It's amazing how God has created our bodies to respond to simple techniques like this!

- *Firm hugs.* Holding a tantrum-throwing child in a gentle-but-firm embrace for at least thirty seconds can help reduce cortisol (which is known as the "stress hormone"), produce a burst of endorphins, and raise dopamine levels. Again, praise God for giving us practical ways to calm our bodies and minds at once! If your child is resistant to this as well, keep in mind that it's your job as his mom to give him the help he needs, even if he doesn't know he needs it. Wrapping a rage-filled child in your arms to keep him from harming belongings, others, or himself, is a kindness that he may only recognize once he is calm.

- *Bullet prayers.* An angry child does not need a lot of words. But short, powerful phrases like "Jesus, help me be calm," "God, help me honor you with my emotions," or "God, you are bigger than my anger" go a long way toward equipping a child who struggles to self-regulate with some tangible things to say to the Lord when he's spiraling.

- *Gratitude.* The last thing a rage-filled child wants to do is admit there is still good in the world. It's natural to want to cling to our annoyance, even as adults. But it helps if we can reframe the frustrating situation, not in terms of what we've lost but instead in terms of things we've gained. I would often ask my precious "rage monster" to "tell me one good thing" once he'd calmed a bit, and, if he could come up with nothing else, he would always default to "I have a family that loves me."

- *Music.* Although I wouldn't lead with this one, if you have a child who has worked through the steps above and still needs a nudge to get back to equilibrium, blasting some upbeat praise and worship music and "dancing it out" is a fantastic way to dispel the last vestiges of "everything is awful."

⟨ DAD THOUGHT ⟩

My older brother and I are very close in age. When we were toddlers, my parents had an understanding that my dad didn't want to deal with little kids but would become involved when we were old enough to do stuff. And by "stuff" he meant play sports and board games and work on projects, *not* throw tantrums, spill every other glass of milk, and scribble "art" on the walls.

Over the years, I've heard similar stories from other families in which dads either openly took a pass on the early years or simply followed in the footsteps of their parents with a "moms provide the nurturing and caretaking while dads provide the money, wisdom, and discipline" philosophy.

It's not that there isn't any validity to this view. As we've already mentioned, having primary roles is a good thing, and our biological differences will better suit us to certain tasks. For many families, this will mean that mothers shoulder the bulk of the more physically demanding and mentally dependent years in their children's lives.

But the tendency of fathers to assume that raising small children is easier for moms (or just harder for dads), and then use that assumption as a reason to excuse themselves from taking part in the "mom jobs," overlooks some very important points:

1. You're probably better suited to digging ditches all day than your wife. But that doesn't mean it would be easy, refreshing, or enjoyable.

2. Even if your wife is more patient and compassionate than you, most toddlers are still hard and a very real emotional and physical drain on her finite well of energy.

3. You have busy seasons at work when everyone wants something from you at once (and yesterday, please), such that you can't simply focus on one thing at a time and get it done. The toddler-raising years are that season in a mama's life, and she needs rest.

4. Husbands are called to love their wives as Christ loved the church (Ephesians 5:25).

5. Christ, in loving the church, calls her to "come to me, all who labor and are heavy laden, and I will give you rest" (Matthew 11:28).

Do we fathers not want the same rest when our jobs are demanding? And are we not in a much better position to give ourselves that rest, considering the greater autonomy many of us have over our schedules? If nothing else, we get government-mandated breaks and can simply walk away when we finish our work for the day. In contrast, toddlers laugh at the thought of a "mandated" break; they're usually up before dawn, fight even the mention of naps or bedtime, and find their way into our wives' side of the bed many nights.

There are many more reasons fathers should help share in the hard that is toddlerdom, but this one is enough by itself: What an opportunity dads have to be imitators of Christ by loving their wives and giving them rest during a season when their load is heavy!

The Narrative

THE WORLD'S RESPONSE TO HARD	A CHRISTIAN RESPONSE TO HARD
Thinks toddlers are "the worst"	Acknowledges that toddlers are both awesome and hard
Fails to take responsibility for setting the tone at home	Recognizes that mothers, not toddlers, are the emotional thermostats of a home
Skimps on consistency and follow-through in favor of a victim mindset	Takes developmental limitations and sin nature into consideration when setting boundaries for little ones

Action Steps

- Memorize and meditate on Galatians 6:9: "And let us not grow weary of doing good, for in due season we will reap, if we do not give up."
- Unfollow accounts that mock and degrade toddlers for their frustrating behaviors.
- Make yourself sticky notes to post around the house (or car) reminding you of the things you love most about the awesome-but-hard little person you are mothering.

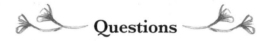

Questions

What are three ways toddlers are awesome? Three ways toddlers are hard? How can God use both to reveal His goodness to us?

Why do some mothers cling so tightly to their right to despise the toddler phase?

How has the Bible called us to view young children?

Prayer

Lord, may Your gracious response of "let the little children come to me and do not hinder them, for to such belongs the kingdom of heaven" (Matthew 19:14) be our guide for how we treat our own toddlers. Give us Your supernatural grace to handle frustrating experiences with wisdom and patience, knowing that You extend those same gifts to us daily.

14

Connecting with Teenagers Is Hard

THE ART OF CHOOSING OUR YESES LAVISHLY AND OUR NOES WISELY

When I was thirteen, I pantsed my friend Beth on the steaming asphalt that doubled as our PE court at the tiny private school that I attended for two years in junior high. She had been tugging on my shorts and cackling every time our PE coach, Mr. G, turned his head, and I was over it. So I tugged back. And her elastic-waisted shorts shot down her nonexistent hips and landed in a puddle at her ankles.

Let's just say I wasn't as stealthy as Beth and landed in the principal's office. Mr. Perryman, an ex-marine with expertly ironed creases in his slacks and a razor-sharp part in his hair, could barely restrain his astonishment when I walked in the door. "Pantsing" wasn't exactly my usual modus operandi. I knew that. All the adults in the room—including my mom, who taught five of my six classes and became aware of my infraction all of seven minutes after it happened—knew it too.

It Never Hurts to Be Cautious

And yet I still received a stern "talking to" and an admonishment to never do it again. I remember staring at my parents in genuine consternation when they both took the time to talk to me again at home about why it was a bad idea.

"Mom, Dad," I said, "it was a terrible idea! But it never occurred to me her pants would actually come *off*. I was just trying to scare her. You don't have to worry about me ever doing that again."

Because they knew it was true, I didn't receive a consequence (other than the embarrassment of entirely too much grown-up attention for the wrong reasons). But as flabbergasted as I was as a young teen at having an out-of-character "blip" addressed with such seriousness, as a mother of multiple teenagers now, I get it.

We hear horror stories about teens eating Tide Pods and dying in agony or getting caught up in an internet phishing scam or undergoing a double mastectomy at fourteen after getting swept into the latest gender confusion trend only to change their minds a year later, and our hearts lurch with panic at all the very real, very imminent dangers that await our precious babies who aren't so babyish anymore.

I can almost picture the wheels in my mom's head turning: "She's been tame up until now, but she's thirteen. What if this pantsing nonsense is just a gateway to more rebellious stuff? Better nip it in the bud now."

I have no idea what she was actually thinking, so maybe that's just a reflection of what my own response would have been, but I do know this: I envy my mother's position of having parented teens in an era of zero smartphones. Long before iPhones existed, the teenage years were already considered one of the more difficult parenting stages to weather, and yet no one but twenty-first-century parents have had to navigate the minefields of Snapchat, TikTok, private chat rooms with disappearing messages within game apps, and Facebook bullying.

It makes me want to cry out with David, "Turn my eyes from looking at worthless things; and give me life in your ways" (Psalm 119:37). And of course, this is what I pray for my teens to desire as well.

An Easy No

I mentioned choosing our "noes" wisely in the subtitle of this chapter, and Shaun and I both agree that one of the easiest noes we have ever chosen is restricting our children's access to social media. They understand—both because they've witnessed it and because we have freely discussed it with them—the difference between the work I do on social media and the time suck that is idly spending hours a day on a variety of apps whose primary end is to distract our minds, capture our hearts, and fill our souls with discontentment, lust, and envy. (Sidenote: the book *12 Ways Your Phone Is Changing You* discusses at length this idea of using smartphones as tools to create value rather than as toys to distract us.)

Can social media be used for good? Absolutely! If we steward it well and are careful to submit first to God whom we follow, what we look at, and what we post, it can be a tool for encouragement, information, and sharing the gospel. But social media can also be a great force for evil, and so we ask our teens to abstain from participating in it with personal accounts until they are adults who pay their own phone bills and fully make their own time-management decisions. (None of our teens have even asked for a private social media account so far.)

By that point, our goal is to have lavished them with so many yeses to good alternatives that time spent alone on screens pales in comparison to evenings filled with Nertz (only the best card game there is), ping-pong tournaments, s'mores on the back patio, games of Risk and Bananagrams, movies on our DIY big screen, chess matches, reading aloud together (yes, my teens still love this), volleyball in the front yard, charades, and—gasp!—even long conversations about whatever strikes their fancy.

If you don't see many things your family enjoys doing together on that list, that's totally fine. Maybe you're more of a sports family or a let's-all-read-books-separately-but-in-the-same-room family or a musical family. I don't know, of course. But the question is: *Do you?* Because if you don't, I highly encourage you to find out.

Taking the time to learn what thrills our children's hearts, and then studying our family time to notice if their passions are reflected there, is crucial to creating a family culture in which our teens want to participate.

Creating a Family Culture Our Teens Crave

Taking the time to learn what thrills our children's hearts, and then studying our family time to notice if their passions are reflected there, is crucial to creating a family culture in which our teens want to participate. This practice of noticing what captures our children's attention starts much earlier than age thirteen, but it's important not to check out, as the nine-year-old once obsessed with all things horses becomes a fifteen-year-old with a thing for hair tutorials.

Too often, our jaded society sells us the lie that our teenagers' minds cannot be captured by anything other than pinging notifications, fifteen-second videos, and viral dance challenges (more on that last bit in a minute). Articles, TV shows, and other parents paint a vivid (and depressing) picture of teens as surly and secretive, resistant to anything sincere, and obsessed with only those things their parents abhor.

I'm aware that all these things *can* be true. And if we haven't already made ourselves students of our children's personalities, preferences, and pitfalls by the time they enter the teen years, scrambling to recover a connection that we lost when we allowed their deepest relationships to form with either peers or technology—or peers *through* technology—will be difficult at best. But there is always hope!

*If we haven't already made ourselves
students of our children's personalities,
preferences, and pitfalls by the time they enter
the teen years, scrambling to recover a connection—
will be difficult at best. But there is always hope!*

As long as our teens live under our roof, we have ample opportunities to discover new ways to connect with their hearts and demonstrate to them that the flesh-and-blood people who live in the same house are their best sources of love, support, and wisdom. But we will not achieve any of these things if we sidestep the hard-but-good tension between still exercising our God-given authority to establish boundaries—for things like social media, dating, internet usage, entertainment, wardrobe decisions, and acceptable speech—and beginning to peel back layers of our influence to allow for the development of their own opinions and, prayerfully, their own relationships with the Lord.

Praying the Right Kind of Prayers

One of our teen boys encountered a significant struggle in his preteen years, and at the time, I wondered why God would allow it to be a part of his story. We prayed, talked, counseled, and disciplined our son through it, but it wasn't until several years later that I was able to fully thank God for the challenge when our son told me that, without it, he might have never truly understood his need for a Savior.

"I didn't really get that *I* was a sinner," he told me. "Just that sin was a thing. This forced me to face my own wrongdoing and ask Jesus to forgive me in a real way for the first time ever."

We had been praying since he was born that he would have a relationship with the Lord separate from our example (ever heard the phrase "God has no grandchildren"?), but if I'd had my way, he would have transitioned seamlessly into owning that relationship without any heartache in the process. I wanted to circumnavigate Hebrews 12:11, which says, "For the moment all discipline seems painful rather than pleasant, but later it yields the peaceful fruit of righteousness to those who have been trained by it."

Interestingly, the Greek word for "discipline" in this verse is *paideia*, which has the idea of "training" or even "rearing a child" (because it's a verse about how God disciplines His children). In other words, raising children *should* be hard and sometimes painful work for both us and our kids, and we should expect to encounter some struggles as we look forward to the "peaceful fruit of righteousness."

Even though we know firsthand how important going through hard things is in helping us to recognize our need for Jesus, we somehow forget this is also true for our children. Because we love them and desire to protect them from harm, we coddle them spiritually with prayers like, "Lord, help him to know You from an early age and never stray from Your path." It's not a bad prayer. But perhaps a better one is, "Lord, do what it takes to get my children's attention and show them their need for You. Send them forth as arrows of light and truth into a dark world that needs bold, biblical, loving followers of Jesus to proclaim and live the gospel with conviction."

A Right Understanding of Rebellion

I was chatting with my friend Kristy, whom I mentioned a few chapters back, about the heartbreak that is young adults who, despite having been faithfully discipled in God's ways, reject the faith of their fathers and mothers for worldly philosophies and "the lust of the flesh, the lust of the eyes, and the pride of life" (1 John 2:16 NKJV). When I mentioned how hard it is on a mother's heart to know she has invested so deeply in her children's lives only to see them reject all that she holds most dear, Kristy said something truly profound: "Yes, it's hard on mothers. But what should truly grieve us is that someone we love is in defiance against *our God*. We cannot allow our feelings or our attachment to make us lose sight of the fact that the true tragedy is our child's rebellion, not against us, but against God."

Phew! That'll preach, friends!

Praise God that He is the only one who can save our kids and that we can only serve as a vehicle for conveying His truth. Still, it's good to self-examine and ask ourselves if we are making the kinds of efforts that honor the Lord and show love to our children.

When we buy into the world's assumption that our teens want nothing to do with us, there's at a least a chance we're not being completely honest about their childhoods. If we looked closely, we might discover that, as young children, they were desperate to be near us, but we channeled their affections in every direction but home because of our own desire for a break, or because of societal pressures to fill our schedules to bursting with extracurriculars, or even because of a mistaken belief that we are foolish and backward-thinking to dread putting our six-week-old baby in daycare so we can return to work. Whatever the reasons for the disconnect from our children, the negative effects can be significant and long-reaching. (And, of course, there are situations in which a relational fissure forms even when a parent has steadily refused to subscribe to any negative assumptions about teenagers.)

All our kids crave our presence, our affection, and our approval. Teens are no different. But if we sidestep their need for connection when they're young, we may long for its return when they are more mentally and physically self-sufficient and choose relationships and guidance elsewhere.

Our kids crave our presence, our affection, and our approval. Teens are no different. But if we sidestep their need for connection when they're young, we may long for its return when they…choose relationships and guidance elsewhere.

Proverbs 1:8-9 says, "Hear, my son, your father's instruction, and forsake not your mother's teaching, for they are a graceful garland for your head and pendants for your neck." Maybe you just snorted at the thought of your teen considering anything you have to say a "graceful garland." Maybe you don't remember the last time you felt anything but intimidated to give your teenager godly advice. Maybe you're worried that you've waited too long and you'll never win their hearts back.

There's Always Hope

Regardless of where you are in your relationship with your teen, I want to encourage you that we serve the God of hope who has the ability to "fill you with all joy and peace in believing, so that by the power of the Holy Spirit you may abound in hope" (Romans 15:13). Parenting hope for the believing Christian is not a delusion but is instead a resolve to trust that things can improve by the grace of God as we persevere in obeying the Lord. If nothing else, *we* can grow in spiritual maturity as we seek to diligently teach God's laws to our children, and "talk of them when you sit in your house, and when you walk by the way, and when you lie down, and when you rise" (Deuteronomy 6:7).

If the thought of literally talking about God's commandments all day feels like it would be too awkward, maybe reframe it this way: How can I reflect God's goodness and truth to my teenagers in all aspects of daily life?

Here are just a few examples.

We can reflect God's love in how we pay attention to what our teens enjoy.

My own mama set a fantastic example of this for me by occasionally taking me on fun dates to Goodwill (where my love of thrifting was born) and then out to eat at Subway (we had very little "extra" money, but she always had coupons) where we would split a twelve-inch sub loaded with turkey, lettuce, tomatoes, onions, green peppers, and pickles (plus banana peppers for her; none for me, thanks). Just listing those ingredients makes my mouth water and brings back a flood of happy memories.

I have a thirteen-year-old daughter who loves "junking" and yummy food just as much as I did at her age, and we sneak away for both, just the two of us, whenever possible.

My seventeen-year-old son loves playing games and eating dessert, so nothing puts a smile on his face more quickly than a fresh-baked treat and a round of ping-pong with me and Shaun.

My fifteen-year-old son has rhythm in his blood, so he and I learned to "shuffle dance" together. We even posted some of our (very amateur) routines to the internet (you can find them using the hashtag #simamashuffles on Instagram).

If just spending time with your teens doing what they love doesn't feel like a proactive way of teaching our kids God's law, Romans 13:8 begs to differ: "Owe no one anything, except to love each other, for the one who loves another has fulfilled the law."

A teen with a full belly and heart is a teen with ears to hear what we have to say.

Not only that, but a teen with a full belly and heart is a teen with ears to hear what we have to say. Some of my best and deepest conversations with my kids have happened while we're riding in the car together on a date, eating frozen custard together, or hitting a ping-pong ball back and forth. It's *why* Deuteronomy 6:7 exhorts us to talk about God's truth all day, every day, wherever we go.

We can reflect God's integrity in the way we practice what we preach.

We love to tease each other in our home, and I will often pretend-fight over the last piece of watermelon or brownie with my older boys, who both tower over me. One day, after Simon cockily proclaimed that he would win in a physical fight with me, Shaun said, "Pretty sure beating your mama up is losing." Simon smirked as Ezra walked by and added, "Big time."

Kind speech and expressions are a nonnegotiable component of our family culture.

While I'm relieved that I've never been in an actual physical altercation with my teenage boys, the truth is that I haven't been in that many verbal ones either. Sure, we've had serious, hard discussions. There have been tones that crossed the line of disrespect. But one thing we've made clear from an early age is that kind speech and expressions are a nonnegotiable component of our family culture *because* we are commanded by Scripture to "be completely humble and gentle; be patient, bearing with one another in love" (Ephesians 4:2 NIV). And we strive to lay a foundation for hard conversation on the kind of relational effort that shows we truly love our children with more than just words (see the first point above about paying attention to their interests).

I know I will get some eye rolls when I say that, for the most part, it doesn't occur to my teenagers to sass their mama. But I also know I'll get a virtual fist bump of solidarity from many mamas who have held a similar line.

Imagine my surprise, then, when Simon came the closest to outright defiance that I've yet to hear from him one night—over eating salad, of all things. It seemed to come out of nowhere as we were finishing up dinner, but even as I reminded him about the principles of respect that we uphold in our home, the Holy Spirit was poking His finger into my side in the most uncomfortable way.

You see, not an hour earlier, Shaun and I had been talking about something that made me feel uneasy, even though in the midst of the conversation I couldn't fully grasp why. The topic of discussion was a bit sensitive, and as I cooked dinner while holding a baby on my hip, and the middle kids loudly played a game close by, my chest began to tighten with anxiety. At some point, Shaun asked what should have been an innocuous question, and I snapped at him in return.

I knew Simon had witnessed the exchange from where he sat on the couch in the living room, and I immediately thought, "I need to apologize to Shaun for letting my stress get the better of me and to Simon for setting a bad example." But before I could draw either of them aside to do so, dinner was in full swing, and Simon had already expressed his disgust for salad with the kind of vehemence that could only mean that his anger had nothing to do with salad at all. We continued with all the necessary cleanup and bedtime routines for the littles, and before I was even done reading *Hank the Cowdog* with Theo and Honor, Simon had settled in a chair nearby to listen, a much calmer expression on his face. As soon as the little boys went to bed, he apologized for his disrespect, ending with "I don't know why I was in such a grouchy mood."

I forgave him, of course, and then asked his forgiveness for setting a bad example of not honoring his father with my words. As I spoke, a grin spread across his face, and he crossed the room to give me a huge hug. His step, as he went off to bed, was light and springy. With a growing suspicion of *why* Simon had felt free to be rude to me, I asked Shaun during our "in-bed check-in" that night whether our son had said anything about my rudeness to his dad. Shaun said that Simon admitted to struggling with the way I had reacted and, whether he realized it or not, was probably "exacting revenge" for my snippiness to his father by being equally rude to me.

I could almost hear the Holy Spirit audibly whisper, "See? You knew what it was all along." What an incredibly humbling way to enforce a truth I already knew: So much more really is "caught than taught" with our children!

I know this is a point about practicing what you preach, but perhaps highlighting a time I did *not* do that well illustrates best that (a) an attitude of "do what I say, not what I do" can only ever end in cognitive dissonance and resentment from our children, and (b) when we do inevitably fall short of accurately mirroring God's integrity, we *always* have the option to repent—to the Lord, to our husbands, and to our kids.

We can reflect God's truth in the way we hold our teens accountable.

Of all the trends I see floating around the child psychology world, one of the most worrisome is the claim that "all emotions are valid." Or its very close counterpart: "There are no bad emotions." I don't expect someone with a secular perspective whose worldview is steeped in postmodern moral relativism to agree with me (although I'm always surprised when some do), but from a biblical perspective, there are multiple untruths tucked into even those two short phrases.

I understand the desire to separate shame from emotions that rise unbidden within us. After all, if we didn't ask for how we feel, how can we label it as either good or bad? Isn't that a bit arbitrary or unfair? Actually, no. The Bible pulls zero punches about addressing the *origin* (namely, the sin-filled human heart) of the emotions we desire to protect or excuse.

Take jealousy for example. Everybody experiences that twinge of green-eyed monster rage at some point in her life. Am I really going to tell you that jealousy is a sin?

Well, even if I won't, James already did. And he wasn't even polite about it. "For where jealousy and selfish ambition exist, there will be disorder and every vile practice" (James 3:16).

Yikes, James! You could stand to take a leaf out of your big brother Jesus's book and just accept people the way they are.

Except Jesus didn't do that either, and the progressive view that Jesus never "judged" anyone is one of the greatest lies we can tell our teens (or anyone else).

Instead, God Incarnate said, "For out of the heart come evil thoughts, murder, adultery, sexual immorality, theft, false witness, slander" (Matthew 15:19). The metaphorical heart He references here has long been considered the source of all human emotion. And yet Jesus's conclusion is not that the unredeemed human heart produces "big feelings" that are neither good nor bad but instead that our hearts can produce a plethora of downright awful things.

Jesus also says, "The good person out of the good treasure of his heart produces good, and the evil person out of his evil treasure produces evil, for out of the abundance of the heart his mouth speaks" (Luke 6:45), and *then* He declares, "No one is good except God alone" (Mark 10:18). In other words, without Jesus as Lord of our hearts, our big feelings get us in big trouble.

 Without Jesus as Lord of our hearts, our big feelings get us in big trouble.

And we see this portrayed to an almost comical (except not) degree in the way the heady cocktail of sin nature and pubescent emotions can cause our teens to prioritize their feelings over logic or self-control. Sometimes I wonder if Proverbs 29:11 was written with a teenager in mind: "A fool vents all his anger, but a wise man holds it back" (BSB). I don't say this because I think all teens are fools. Far from it. But they are going through a *lot* of body and brain changes in a short amount of time, which often results in foolish choices.

Plus, they are discovering so many things they desire that they just aren't ready to use responsibly and righteously (like sex, credit cards, and fast, shiny cars). Throw in the fact that "desire when it has conceived gives birth to sin, and sin when it is fully grown brings forth death" (James 1:15), and it can feel a bit like there's no chance of helping our teenagers stay on the straight and narrow.

Yet that is exactly what Deuteronomy 6:7 calls parents to do. We were once teenagers. We understand the struggle. We have faced the same choices. And now, as sanctified adults (who still sin but are no longer slaves to it), we are equipped with biblical truth, experience, godly wisdom, and even a commission from the Lord not to give our teenagers a pass for giving full vent to everything they feel but to lovingly call them to repentance and provide consequences when the situation warrants.

We cannot do this well if we have not first built a relationship of trust by demonstrating an avid interest in them as individuals loved first by God—and by proving that we will hold ourselves to a high standard of emotional self-control and biblical truth.

Or as a pithy saying I've seen floating around the internet puts it:

Rules without relationship = rebellion.

Relationship without rules = chaos.

Relationship + rules = respect and responsibility.

(Or at least it *should*.)

If our teens are not followers of Christ, so much of how we interact with them will be a testimony to the transforming power of the gospel in our own lives. We cannot preach truth to them if we do not believe it or obey it ourselves.

A fool vents
all his anger,
but a wise man
holds it
back.

PROVERBS 29:11
(BSB)

And we cannot coddle our own ungodly emotions when Colossians 3:5-8 so clearly commands this:

> Put to death therefore what is earthly in you: sexual immorality, impurity, passion, evil desire, and covetousness, which is idolatry. On account of these the wrath of God is coming. In these you too once walked, when you were living in them. But now you must put them all away: anger, wrath, malice, slander, and obscene talk from your mouth.

Connecting with teenagers can be hard, y'all. Many of the loudest voices in our culture will tell us it's impossible because teenage brains have taken a vacation and won't come home for many years. Maybe we can attempt a relationship again once they've returned to reason—often after making so many ungodly choices that their lives are forever damaged.

But the Bible gives us hope that truth is not limited to a particular age group. After all, Paul exhorts Timothy to "let no one despise you for your youth, but set the believers an example in speech, in conduct, in love, in faith, in purity" (1 Timothy 4:12). And if you've ever wondered, "How can a young man keep his way pure?" Psalm 119:9 has the answer: "By guarding it according to your [God's] word."

By praying for, teaching God's Word to, investing in, and unconditionally loving our young men and women, we can help them have the kind of unshakeable biblical confidence that empowers them to ward off the barrage of ungodly, confusing, anxiety-inducing messaging from worldly culture. It is our privilege to be their guide as they inch closer and closer to full-fledged adulthood.

Don't buy into the narrative that teenagers are hopeless, friends. I have three so far who—while far from perfect, just like their mama—are some of my favorite people on the planet, and I cannot wait to see how the Lord uses their unique stories to impact the world for His kingdom. It's a lot of hard work planting seeds of relationship *and* boundaries, but my goodness, how sweet the fruit can be!

DAD THOUGHT

My dad made good on his "deal" with my mom from the last chapter to become more involved in our lives as we matured out of the "hard" years. Though he is a man of few words and not one to impart fatherly advice, we enjoyed games, worked on projects, played sports, watched movies, and read books. He set an example of steadiness, selflessness, and hard work throughout bankruptcy, night classes, career changes, and my mother's struggles with mental illness.

Such was the strength of my bond with him that, upon leaving for college, I found myself a deist, just like my father, despite my mother's faith and years in church and despite my dad's never having tried to share his own beliefs or dissuade me from Christianity.

And here we get to the point: Just as with the parable of the sower in Matthew 13, the instruction we sow in our children's hearts and minds, whether explicitly spoken or implicitly shown, needs fertile ground in which to take hold.

The relationship we share with our child is the ground upon which we sow, and each kind word, joyful moment, struggle, act of forgiveness, thoughtful gift, spontaneous outing, encouragement, achievement—each experience shared in love—adds a layer of richness and depth to that soil. If we fail to "prep the soil" with this warm-hearted engagement, our kids will often receive our instruction as cool and distant, quickly forgotten or, worse yet, a "noisy gong or clanging cymbal" (1 Corinthians 13:1).

My father built that relationship with me, but he failed to sow it with instruction apart from the example he set. He loved, but he did not train or teach. So it was that after years at college away from his example, I found myself disillusioned with the distant god of deism and craving personal direction and wisdom. And here, the Lord grew those seeds my mother planted when I was young. He left the ninety-nine to bring this sheep back into the fold where I found the fatherly guidance and wisdom that surpasses anything my earthly father could have provided.

I think we all crave a deep relationship with a wise counselor. Our kids will look to us first for that connection, but if we neglect to fill the role, they will inevitably seek it elsewhere. Of course we won't (and shouldn't) be the only influences in our children's lives. But when they go looking to fill a void we have failed to tend with love, it leaves them vulnerable to the allure of worldly relationships and unbiblical messaging, which can only lead through the wide gate of destruction (Matthew 7:13).

Wisdom without warmth may drive our children away. Warmth without wisdom may fail to point our children to Christ.

We will never get it all perfectly right, but if we are intentional to invest in developing a relationship our children *want* to engage in—*and* add to it both an example and instruction rooted in God's Word—we will provide them a deep and fertile soil, ready to fuel their growth and faith in the Wonderful Counselor whose love and direction *are* perfect.

The Narrative

THE WORLD'S RESPONSE TO HARD	A CHRISTIAN RESPONSE TO HARD
Says "Just you wait until they're teens!"	Believes that every stage has its unique joys and challenges
Majors on rules without relationship (or relationship without rules)	Understands that connecting with teens is the best way to establish and enforce meaningful boundaries
Gets swept away in a torrent of teen hormones and "big emotions"	Knows that God gave us and our teens biblical truth to trump and balance emotions and hormones

Action Steps

- Memorize and meditate on Romans 13:8: "Owe no one anything, except to love each other, for the one who loves another has fulfilled the law."
- Make a list of three things your teenager(s) love(s). Put them on your calendar this week.
- Ask your accountability partner to pray for your resolve to preach truth to your teens, a genuine desire to show love to your teens, and perseverance to be a consistent Christlike model for your teens.

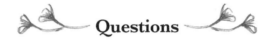

Questions

How does the world's view of "teenagerdom" differ from the Bible's exhortations to young adults (especially in Proverbs)?

What are three ways that teenagers are awesome? Three ways they're hard? How can the Lord use both for good in our lives?

How would viewing my teen as a future peer (and hopefully sister or brother in Christ)—and taking responsibility for the influence I have on them—change my treatment of them or attitude toward them now?

Prayer

*Lord, You love our teens, even when we struggle to like them
sometimes. You encourage us not to look down on young men
and women simply because they are young (1 Timothy 4:12), and
You exhort us to be patient with everyone, "bearing with one
another in love" (Ephesians 4:2). Help us to see our teens with
Your eyes and invest in them with care and intentionality.*

HARD IS NOT THE SAME THING AS BAD

15

Motherhood
Is Hard

REJECTING A MARTYR COMPLEX
TO CHOOSE TRUE JOY

I could write a chapter about the unique challenges of every single phase of mothering and receive no end of support, nods of agreement, and commiseration.

Devoting three chapters to particularly hot-button stages in no way negates the fact that we will at times feel flummoxed by our elementary-aged kids (I have never encountered a toddler tantrum that even remotely competes with an episode of rage over *folding washcloths* that one of our seven-year-olds once indulged in), our preteens (oy, with the "I have no idea why I'm crying" moments!), and even our adult children (I'm not *quite* there yet, but I can only imagine how hard my own mother has bitten her tongue over some of my choices as a young mom).

The Perspective Shift That Changes the Way We Mother

The common denominator—other than the ever-present challenges—is the fact that every stage has the possibility of producing so much joy and maturity in our lives as Bible-believing Christian mamas. And the deciding factor of whether the emotional scales will tip in the direction of "This is so hard! I hate it!" or "This is worth the effort! I am grateful I get to do this!" is almost always the perspective with which we view the struggle.

We have the choice to see only the negative in the hard things we encounter in parenting. And we will confront so many opportunities in person and online to be sucked into this thought pattern.

One dad of teenagers wanted to "comfort" his internet readers with the "sage" advice that "If you think the toddler stage is hard, just wait. It only gets worse."

Another "mommy snark" blogger needed to know if all her followers considered their ten-year-olds just as big of "a pain in the a**" as she did. Hundreds of comments on the post assured her that she was not alone in despising her preteen, while dozens more bemoaned the future: "Wait, you're telling me my $%#& of a six-year-old *isn't* already as bad as she's going to be?!"

Yahoo published a cache of posts with the headline "Funniest Parenting Tweets on the Internet Right Now."

Among them: "The 'Terrible Twos' are a total lie. Because the truth is that ages three, four, five are 'terrible too.'"

I could go on and on, but I think you get the point.

Whenever I encounter such determinedly toxic views of children, I usually conclude two things:

1. This is how these parents really feel about their kids. They wouldn't post this if there weren't at least a kernel of truth to their annoyance.

2. They're also posting this because it "sells." A quick scroll through the enthusiastically nasty responses proves that if you're looking for soaring engagement levels, complaining about your kids is a surefire way to get them.

Of course, the question is: Why is Conclusion Number Two the way the world is? Why does tearing down and degrading children appeal to so many (including self-proclaimed Christians)? *Especially* in light of Matthew 18:10, which says, "See that you do not despise one of these little ones. For I tell you that in heaven their angels always see the face of my Father who is in heaven."

God's Ways Are Not Our Ways

The most obvious answer is something we've already talked about in the last two chapters: sin nature. Our sinful flesh wants a good outcome without the pain of working for it. And when we don't get it, watch out. We will make our disappointment known!

Also, we want to know that, if we do put the work in, it will matter—that we will have an impact on eternity, and we will have it on our terms and in our timing.

Ecclesiastes 3:9-11 (BSB) says, "What does the worker gain from his toil? I have seen the burden that God has laid upon the sons of men to occupy them. He has made everything beautiful in its time. He has also set eternity in the hearts of men, yet they cannot fathom the work that God has done from beginning to end."

God, the Creator, has imbued humankind with a longing for eternity. We innately sense that we were made for more than this earth with its temporal hurt and happiness. But we also grapple with the effects of the fall and the desire for perpetual ease that lives in our own selfish hearts. We "cannot fathom the work that God has done from beginning to end." We see only snatches of His purposes and methods.

I am convinced this is a good thing. If I'd known when I was a twenty-three-year-old, freaked-out, first-time mama that the Lord was going to grace me with ten children, it would have added to my stress, not diminished it.

Thankfully, "he has made everything beautiful in its time." The family God planned for me and Shaun is the most beautiful gift either of us has ever received, and we are overjoyed to be granted the responsibility to parent our crew. (Truly! Even when they drive us bonkers!) But it happened in God's time and in His way.

In 2019, our family spent months planning and budgeting for a once-in-a-lifetime trip to Europe to cap off our 2020 homeschool year. When I found out I was pregnant in January of 2020, one of my very practical concerns was the prospect of keeping up with the rest of our eight kids in the streets of Paris while pregnant, sick, and tired.

And *then* we found out we were pregnant with not one boy but two, Titus *and* Toby, and my mindset morphed from "keeping up" to "waddling slowly behind." Twin pregnancies are difficult, to put it mildly, and this one ended up being especially hard. I found myself questioning God's timing and wisdom in giving us double blessings with such a big trip looming.

And then—surprise twist—international travel to Europe was suspended because of COVID-19 mere weeks before we were scheduled to board our airplane to London. And it became oh-so-clear that I had been worrying about something the Lord knew was never going to happen. Just like Proverbs 16:9 says, "The heart of man plans his way, but the LORD establishes his steps."

Were we wrong to plan that trip a year in advance? I don't believe so. We prayed for wisdom and took all the practical steps needed while still striving to hold a James 4:15 attitude of "if the Lord wills." And ultimately, when the Lord clearly did not have that trip in store for us, we experienced disappointment, yes, but also supernatural peace in trusting His perfect will.

Expectation that things are "supposed" to go a certain way will often result in disillusionment.

And that, friends, is so often the difference between an attitude of bitterness and a posture of contentment when it comes to our kids. An expectation that things are "supposed" to go a certain way will often result in disillusionment (when the toddler starts running a high fever after we've already packed the car for our weekend away with our husband) or sometimes even devastation (when the little boy whose football career Dad was already planning in utero is born with a condition that means he'll never walk).

There Is No Formula

There is no formula to ensure that our kids "turn out" a certain way—emotionally, mentally, spiritually, or physically. And trying to apply one, instead of continually giving them back to God with a posture of "They've always been Yours anyway," produces so much frustration and resentment.

We see it in the unfortunate internet posts I mentioned above. We see it in our own hearts when we long for a hard phase to be done, only to find ourselves angrily facing a different but equally difficult season.

I have so much respect for Hannah in the Old Testament. In the midst of infertility and the pain of witnessing her husband's other wife not only being able to bear children but also mocking Hannah for her lack, Hannah cries out to the Lord for the mercy of a child.

God hears and answers her prayer with a healthy baby boy named Samuel. If I were Hannah, I think I would have love-smothered that long-awaited baby with my hovering attention. Far from being a helicopter parent, though, Hannah makes good on the oath she swore to the Lord that if He gave her a child, she would devote him back to God when he was weaned. In 1 Samuel 1:28 (NIV), Hannah brings her little son to the temple to present to the priest, Eli, saying, "I give him to the LORD. For his whole life he will be given over to the LORD."

We don't know of any promise the Lord has given her that she will receive the favor of more children. And yet she trusts Him. And in return, He blesses her faith richly with three sons and two daughters after Samuel.

Hannah understood that raising children to the glory of God is a holy mission straight from Him—one to which we should be wholly devoted *while* holding the outcome loosely. I want to emulate her example! But it is only by focusing on eternity and seeking help from the Lord that I can avoid getting bogged down by the sheer incessancy of being needed every waking (and sometimes sleeping) moment of the day.

We Are Not Martyrs to Motherhood

We've touched on this concept already, but it bears repeating that it is easy (and tempting) to succumb to an attitude of Motherhood Martyrdom—to believe that our children are keeping us from more than they are giving us. If you think I'm exaggerating, look no further than this quote from Glennon Doyle, the woman *People* magazine declared "the patron saint of female empowerment." In her book *Untamed* she says,

> Mothers have martyred themselves in their children's names since the beginning of time. We have lived as if she who disappears the most, loves the most. We have been conditioned to prove our love by slowly ceasing to exist. What a terrible burden for children to bear—to know that they are the reason their mother stopped living.

Doyle is a self-described "Christian mommy blogger." I cannot claim to know the state of her heart, but I do know she openly denies basic tenets of biblical truth, including God's plan for marriage between one man and one woman laid out in Genesis 2:24 (Doyle is married to a woman after divorcing her husband of over a decade), God's plan for a binary view of gender that starts and ends with male and female (Genesis 5:2), and most notably, as seen in her book quote above, Jesus's declaration, "If anyone would come after me, let him deny himself and take up his cross and follow me" (Matthew 16:24).

Clearly, she does not write that children are "the reason their mother stopped living" because she believes this is a good thing. And in this, if not much else, she and I agree. If we take up our crosses and deny ourselves daily for the sake of our children alone, we will have missed the whole point. But if we deny ourselves and take up our crosses for Jesus's sake and, *in that process*, serve our families in a way that mirrors His sacrifice for us, we will have understood the assignment.

It is a crucial distinction but one that I doubt Doyle would appreciate, since her point seems to be that mothers who appear to diminish in any individual capacity have done so not out of obedience to Christ but as a result of societal pressure. But when we place the concept of proving our love "by slowly ceasing to exist" beside Christ's standard of "Thy will be done" (Matthew 6:10

KJV)—before our own interests, our own preferences, or our own passions—we see that while the former could indeed be the response to cultural conditioning, the latter is a wildly *countercultural* call to action that clashes with our current climate of self-obsession and self-deification.

Doyle—with the support of the thousands of women who read and find validation in her books—is calling for the ultimate secular motherhood intervention: enlightening women about the "foolishness" of self-denial in light of what she sees as their inherent power and self-worth.

Doyle goes on: "If we keep passing down the legacy of martyrdom to our daughters, with whom does it end? Which woman ever gets to live? And when does the death sentence begin? At the wedding altar? In the delivery room? Whose delivery room—our children's or our own?"

Dead to Self, Alive to Christ

Scripture, however, asks not, "Which woman ever gets to live?" but instead, "Who is willing to die to herself?" The latter is an eternally minded question that is all the more impactful for the paradoxical beauty of the answer we find in the following verses:

- "For whoever would save his life will lose it, but whoever loses his life for my sake will save it. For what does it profit a man if he gains the whole world and loses or forfeits himself?" (Luke 9:24-25).

- "Now if we have died with Christ, we believe that we will also live with him" (Romans 6:8).

- "You were taught, with regard to your former way of life, to put off your old self, which is being corrupted by its deceitful desires; to be made new in the attitude of your minds; and to put on the new self, created to be like God in true righteousness and holiness" (Ephesians 4:22-24 NIV).

- "Those who belong to Christ Jesus have nailed the passions and desires of their sinful nature to his cross and crucified them there.

Since we are living by the Spirit, let us follow the Spirit's leading in every part of our lives" (Galatians 5:24-25 NLT).

- "I have been crucified with Christ and I no longer live, but Christ lives in me" (Galatians 2:20 NIV).

- "He [Jesus] must increase, but I must decrease" (John 3:30).

Modern mom culture, as exemplified by Doyle's (and so many others') words, preaches that choosing to pour ourselves out for our families is a "death sentence" that begins at the wedding altar or in the delivery room, and only by pursuing "self" will we be fulfilled and ultimately free our daughters from a future of self-denial.

Friends, without the transforming power of the Holy Spirit in our lives, few of us could resist the shimmering appeal of the logic that says, "Putting yourself first is the only way to authentically love anyone else."

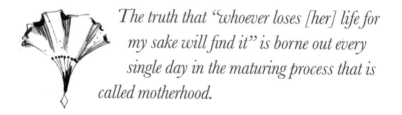

The truth that "whoever loses [her] life for my sake will find it" is borne out every single day in the maturing process that is called motherhood.

And yet with the Holy Spirit as our guide, we can plainly see the truth that "whoever loses [her] life for my sake will find it" is borne out every single day in the maturing process that is called motherhood.

But don't take my word for it. Here are just a few of the hundreds of responses I received from readers when I asked them about their most profound hard-but-good insights from motherhood.

- "Without the hard, I may sadly go through life without the blaring realization of my own need for a Savior."

- "In this hard season of faithfully seeking to be consistent in discipline and child-training, the Lord provides opportunity after opportunity to rehearse the gospel together."

- "Getting to be exhausted at the end of the day. I consider it a blessing! I can remember, in my less responsible days, not being able to put my mind or my body to rest. I find rest in Him and am grateful for my able mind and body."

- "Sleep deprivation. Going from anger to gratefulness that I have so many sweet reasons to be sleep deprived."

- "Breastfeeding can be so hard and painful and can even feel impossible, but it is so worth it and is such a sweet, selfless act that bonds you with your child like nothing else I've experienced."

- "The noise can be deafening, but in those moments, if I take just a minute to lean into the Lord, His comfort and promises are louder."

- "The time sacrifice can be hard but also the most rewarding. Saying no to the things the culture has ingrained in our mind that we, as moms, 'deserve.' My oldest is sixteen and so close to flying the coop. I have never looked back and thought, 'I sure wish I'd spent less time with her and more time on myself.'"

- "Being a mom has taught me more about serving others in the way that Jesus did than anything else in my life."

I wish I could share all their insights with you, friends, because they were that good, but alas, I find myself near the end of my allotted ink and paper.

A Benediction for Steadfast Moms

Being a mother is hard. Anyone who says otherwise is living in a fantasy world.

But it's equally as fanciful to insist that, just because something is hard, we should avoid it or despise it. And it's even more unrealistic to assume that something as rich in investment and reward as raising children should be easy.

First Peter 4:12-13 says, "Beloved, do not be surprised at the fiery trial when it comes upon you to test you, as though something strange were happening to you. But rejoice insofar as you share Christ's sufferings, that you may also rejoice and be glad when his glory is revealed."

No hardship we encounter in motherhood can compare to the excruciating pain and isolation of the cross, but every time we choose to lean into a challenge, whether merely distasteful or soul crushing, we are privileged to share a tiny portion of Christ's sufferings *and* His glory.

It is both this privilege and this glory that spur us to "press on toward the goal for the prize of the upward call of God in Christ Jesus" (Philippians 3:14).

I may not ever encounter a phase of motherhood that feels completely effortless. At this point, I hope I don't. I enjoy and praise God for the easier seasons just as much as the next girl. But I learn from and become more Christlike because of the hard ones. So I refuse to wish them away.

Maybe you feel the same, so I'll leave you with this little benediction:

May the God of peace fill every mother's heart with assurance in the knowledge that she has carried Jesus's easy yoke and light burden well as her head droops with exhaustion on her pillow each night. May His joy flood our spirits with gratitude for the children who leave marks of our deep mother's love for them on our bodies and souls. And may Christ's sacrifice for our sins ever and always be the ultimate reminder that hard is not the same thing as bad.

Amen.

PRESS ON TOWARD THE GOAL FOR THE PRIZE OF THE UPWARD CALL OF GOD IN CHRIST JESUS.

PHILIPPIANS 3:14

 **The Narrative**

THE WORLD'S RESPONSE TO HARD	A CHRISTIAN RESPONSE TO HARD
Views motherhood as a martyrdom from which to escape as often as possible	Sees motherhood as an opportunity to live out Jesus's call to lose our lives so that we may find them
Mocks kids as a form of "stress relief"	Knows that "death and life are in the power of the tongue" and guards our mouths against snark
Resents all that motherhood has "stolen" from us	Finds in motherhood immeasurable opportunities to identify with Christ in His sufferings *and* joys

 **Action Steps**

- Memorize and meditate on Philippians 3:14: "Press on toward the goal for the prize of the upward call of God in Christ Jesus."

- Write out a "Mama Manifesto"—a statement of truth about what kind of mother you are (or desire to be) and why. Take your time on this. You want it to be something you can prayerfully return to on hard mothering days to remind you why the effort and sacrifice are all worth it.

- Make a list of three things that you have "found" in "losing yourself" to motherhood.

Questions

What hard-but-good insight(s) would you add to the list that I shared from my readers?

Why is an attitude of martyrdom in motherhood so antithetical to what Scripture teaches us about dying to self?

What are three specific ways that God is calling you "toward the goal for the prize of the upward call of God"?

Prayer

Lord, it is a privilege and a blessing to lose ourselves to be found in You. Thank You for the opportunity each day to share in Your sufferings and joys through the calling of motherhood. Clarify our vision to see the truth of what an honor it is to be called "Mama."

Acknowledgments

Jennifer, you are the best editor-who-isn't-officially-an-editor that a girl could ask for. Your unflagging encouragement, cheerleading, and reminders to put my punctuation *inside* freestanding parenthetical statements have made a world of difference in my writing. Lindsay, you've done it again. Kind of can't believe I'm best friends with an artist who has such an uncanny ability to take the images in my head and make them come alive so exquisitely on the page. Mama, thanks for wrangling babies every Wednesday afternoon (and plenty more) so I could bang out a chapter or two. Heather, thanks for trusting me and understanding when I need "hands off" and when I need a good talking-to. Shaun, you know what you do, and you do it so well. Really, really. (P.S. It was so fun to write with you. Let's do it again sometime!)

Notes

50   **He is no fool:** Jim Elliot, *The Journals of Jim Elliot* (Ada, MI: Baker Publishing Group, 2002).

50   **There is no safer place:** Corrie ten Boom, *Each New Day* (Ada, MI: Revell, 1977).

51, 55   **Tragedy had struck** and **The everlasting arms:** Cited in Don Pucik, "Insight: Casper ten Boom on Suffering for Him," EquippingSaints.com, January 7, 2020, https://equippingsaints.com/2020/01/07/insight-casper-ten -boom-on-suffering-for-him/. From Corrie Ten Boom, *Father Ten Boom* (Old Tappan, NJ: Fleming H. Revell Company, 1973).

61   **1.35 million deaths:** "Road Traffic Injuries and Deaths—A Global Problem," Centers for Disease Control and Prevention, January 10, 2023, https://www .cdc.gov/injury/features/global-road-safety/index.html.

68   **Sometimes when we:** This quote is widely attributed to Elisabeth Elliot and is thought to be from one of her radio broadcasts.

102   **When you write:** From a slide on the Instagram account @hopewriters.

112   **To be a Christian:** C.S. Lewis, "The Weight of Glory," *Theology* 43, no. 257 (1941): 263–74.

115   **The scars you share:** Jon Acuff, "The Scars Are Lighthouses," *Stuff Christians Like* (blog), December 4, 2013, https://stuffchristianslike.net/2013/12/04 /scars-lighthouses/.

133   **He never made a fuss:** Elisabeth Elliot, first published in *Guided by God's Promises*, https://elisabethelliot.org/resource-library/devotionals /jesus-was-never-busy/.

230, 231 **Mothers have martyred** and **If we keep passing:** Glennon Doyle, *Untamed* (New York: The Dial Press, 2020), 128.

About Abbie

Abbie Halberstadt is a happy wife and mama of ten children, including two sets of identical twins. She's also a homeschool educator, fitness instructor, business owner, speaker, writer, and reigning family Nertz champion. Abbie lives by the motto that "hard is not the same thing as bad." Through her blog and social media posts, she encourages women to dig deep to meet the challenges of everyday life. She, her husband, Shaun, and their children live in the Piney Woods of East Texas.

In her first book, *M Is for Mama*, Abbie invites like-minded moms to join the rebellion against mediocre motherhood and aspire to more than the current cultural standard of merely surviving another day of child raising with the empty validation of fist bumps and snarky memes.

Abbie shares advice, encouragement, and scripturally sound strategies—seasoned with humor and grace—to help you embrace the challenges and see the many rewards of Christlike motherhood.

Are you ready to join the rebellion?
Visit misformama.net to learn more.